DATE DUE

Guidelines for Family Support Practice

F A M I L Y   R E S O U R C E S   C O A L I T I O N

Published 1996

Printed in the United States of America.

00 99 98 97   10 9 8 7 6 5 4 3 2

Library of Congress Cataloging in Publication Data

Guidelines for family support practice.
        p.   cm.—(Guidelines for effective practice)
    Includes bibliographical references
    ISBN 1-885429-14-2 (alk. paper)
    1. Family allowances—United States—Handbooks,
manuals, etc. 2. Aid to families with dependent children
programs—United States—Handbooks, manuals, etc.
I. Best Practices Project (Family Resource Coalition)
II. Series.
HV699.G85   1996   96-26929
362.82' 82—dc20   CIP

For additional copies of this book or to receive a catalog of
publications related to family support, contact Family Resource
Coalition, 200 South Michigan Avenue, 16th Floor, Chicago,
IL 60604, 312/341-0900 (phone) or 312/341-9361 (fax).

CONTENTS

Preface
page v

Acknowledgments
page vii

Chapter 1
THE FAMILY SUPPORT STORY
page 1

Chapter 2
RELATIONSHIP BUILDING
page 9

Chapter 3
ENHANCING FAMILY CAPACITY
page 29

Chapter 4
AFFIRMING DIVERSITY
page 49

Chapter 5
PROGRAMS IN COMMUNITIES
page 71

Chapter 6
PROGRAM PLANNING, GOVERNANCE, AND ADMINISTRATION
page 93

Chapter 7
LOOKING TO THE FUTURE
page 113

Appendix A
RECOMMENDED RESOURCES
page 117

Appendix B
THE BEST PRACTICES PROJECT
page 119

Appendix C
PREMISES AND PRINCIPLES OF FAMILY SUPPORT
page 131

For some time, guidelines for effective practice in the fast-growing field of family support have been needed. Family support programs have proliferated quickly in many different settings in response to an increasing emphasis in the public policy arena on a family support strategy. Efforts to establish benchmarks that measure quality in programs and a framework for training practitioners have been hampered by the lack of a widely accepted definition of effective practice. Efforts to successfully incorporate a family support approach into large public systems have been impeded because there has been no clear articulation of principles to be followed.

A group of family support leaders convened at a Wingspread conference in fall, 1991 to discuss a conceptual framework for training in family support. At their urging, the Family Resource Coalition undertook to develop a definition of best practices in family support programs. The Best Practices Project Steering Committee was appointed by the Family Resource Coalition Board of Directors in summer 1992; its members represent a variety of perspectives on current practice in the field.

From the beginning, the Best Practices Project called for extensive participation from local family support practitioners in defining best practice in the field. Local practitioners are considered to be the best possible source of knowledge about practice in their own programs. While these programs do not represent all of the settings in which family supportive practice occurs today, they possess many years of experience in implementing the theories that underlie today's practice. The diversity and longevity of experience that they bring to the process of defining practice in the field are essential to obtaining a credible result.

All programs that were included in the Family Resource Coalition database were invited to participate in the project by holding facilitated focus groups for both staff and parents participating in their programs. More than 350 programs responded enthusiastically to the invitation, and more than 2,000 people ultimately participated in the project. Each focus group reported extensively on how the principles of family support were carried out in its program. For many programs, the focus groups offered a unique opportunity to discuss principles behind their practice in depth. Many reported that the experience of holding focus groups had challenged them to look at their practice in a new way and to make improvements in what they were doing.

The data collected from the focus groups was analyzed under the direction of the Analysis Team of the Best Practices Project Steering Committee. This information from the field formed the basis for this book. The practices discussed in *Guidelines for Family Support Practice* represent good practices that exist in hundreds of programs around the country, not necessarily what the future of family support may look like or what research may eventually tell us is the most effective way to work. The original principles used in the focus groups have now been re-drafted to reflect input from local programs about what constitutes good practice at this point in time.

Other important contributions to the project came from recognized experts in the field. A paper summarizing the characteristics of existing community-based family support programs was commissioned from family support expert Carl Dunst as a starting point for the project. Additional papers were commissioned by FRC to further explore specific aspects of family support practice that are still emerging: family support in early childhood programs (by Mary Larner), the contribution of family support programs to child protection (by Joyce Thomas, forthcoming), and the potential of family support programs to further the goal of cultural democracy (by Makungu Akinyela, forthcoming). The papers are important complements to *Guidelines for Family Support Practice*, and the ideas expressed in them are reflected throughout the book. The papers are available or forthcoming from the Family Resource Coalition.

The final result of the Best Practices Project, *Guidelines for Family Support Practice* represents a consensus among practitioners in the field about good practice in family support programs.

These guidelines are meant to be a beginning point for further development, not the last word on best practices in a field that is changing rapidly and has been the subject of relatively little rigorous program evaluation. The project's steering committee decided that in the current phase of development in the field, without more evidence than is currently available about the results of practice, it would be inappropriate to use the term "best practices" in the book's title. In addition, the responsive nature of family support programs requires them to adapt constantly to the changing needs of the families and communities they serve. "Best practice" at one point in time, with one kind of family, may not be best practice in a different situation. Developing a set of universal premises and principles, with specific guidelines for how they are manifested in the field, ultimately became the goal of the Best Practices Project. *Guidelines for Family Support Practice* is a starting point for further refinement, discussion, and evaluation as the field grows, and exemplifies a consensus on the state of the art today.

(See appendix B for more information on how the Best Practices Project and *Guidelines for Family Support Practice* were developed.)

Guidelines for Family Support Practice is the culmination of a multi-year effort on the part of the Family Resource Coalition's Best Practices Project, which sought to identify, define, and articulate quality practice in the field of family support.

Since its inception, this project has benefited from an unprecedented level of collaboration and commitment among practitioners, family participants in programs, scholars, and advocates of family support. More than 2,000 staff and family participants of family support programs throughout the U.S. and in Canada contributed many hours and resources in order to provide information and insight based on their experience and expertise. Their commitment and contributions are greatly appreciated.

The project has been chaired by Douglas Powell of Purdue University and Bernice Weissbourd, FRC President, who have generously shared their experience and wisdom. They rolled up their sleeves and "dug into" the work of facilitating meetings of the Best Practices Project Steering Committee, advising FRC staff, writing sections of the manuscript, and extensively reviewing and editing drafts. Douglas Powell spent a great deal of time and energy carefully reviewing and making recommendations on the Best Practices Project commissioned papers *Linking Family Support and Early Childhood Programs* by Mary Larner and *Key Characteristics and Features of Community-Based Family Support Programs* by Carl Dunst. In sum, Douglas Powell and Bernice Weissbourd, as steering committe co-chairs, saw the entire process through, from beginning to end, providing unflagging leadership, dedication, insight, and critical analysis.

Their efforts were supported by a steering committee comprised of insightful and experienced thinkers and workers in the field of family support: Hedy Nai-Lin Chang, Maria Chavez, Moncrieff Cochran, Carl Dunst, Emily Fenichel, Jeanne Jehl, Sharon Lynn Kagan, Karen Kelley-Ariwoola, Ricardo La Foré, Delores Norton, Maria Elena Orrego, Linda Passmark, Sharon Peregoy, Karen Pittman, Maisha Sullivan, and Sheila Sussman. The steering committee shepherded the project and painstakingly reviewed all of its output. In addition, a sub-committee of the steering committee, the Analysis Team, analyzed all of the data collected by the project. Members of this "A-Team" included: Hedy Nai-Lin Chang, Maria Chavez, Moncrieff Cochran, Dolores Norton, Karen Pittman, and steering committee co-chairs Douglas Powell and Bernice Weissbourd.

The leaders of FRC's African American and Latino Caucuses have made the Best Practices Project one of their priorities and have offered their insight and efforts towards assuring both quality and inclusiveness.

The first research phase of the project was extensive and inclusive. Many FRC staff members contributed to the comprehensive literature review, to gleaning information from materials received from local programs, and to conducting interviews with local practitioners. Under the guidance of FRC Executive Director Judy Langford Carter, Lourdes Sullivan led this effort as Best Practices Project Coordinator. She worked tirelessly to ensure that the process was true to its values and its goals of inclusiveness, intellectual honesty and rigor, and cultural democracy. She was assisted to varying extents by then–FRC staff members Karen Kelley-Ariwoola, Carolyn Ash, Edith Crigler, Paul Deane, Diane Halbrook, Kai Jackson, Stephanie Lubin, Olga Nieto, Lynn Pooley, and Layla Suleiman. Consultants David Diehl and Shep Zeldin; interns Sylvia Aguilera, Lauren Brown, Ruby Mendenhall, and Armida Ornelas; and a number of administrative support staff all played important roles.

In the final research and writing stages, Judy Langford Carter and Kathy Goetz Wolf turned the process into a document, serving as principal writers and editors. They organized existing materials, met with experts to fill in informational gaps, and worked ceaselessly to assure that the document fulfilled its promise. Kathy Goetz Wolf took primary responsibility for compiling, developing, and writing the Guidelines for Practice sections of the chapters (and for managing and supervising the editing, review, design, and production of the book). The introductory section of chapter 4 was drafted by Hedy Nai-Lin Chang. Judy Langford Carter wrote all other portions of the manuscript, based on extensive drafts prepared by Lourdes Sullivan. Charles Bruner of the Child and Family Policy Center in Iowa; Blanca Almonte, Maureen Patrick, and Delores Holmes of Family Focus, Inc.; Portia Kennel of the Ounce of Prevention Fund; and Lina Cramer provided important information and review at crucial junctures. Steering committee and A-Team members Moncrieff Cochran, Emily Fenichel, and Sharon Lynn Kagan made essential contributions during the research and writing. FRC staff members Nilofer Ahsan, Jill Garcia, Jacqueline Lalley, Mark McDaniel, Shelley Peck, Lynn Pooley, Shamara Riley, Brenda Rodriguez, and Bryan Samuels and intern Sharon Fox contributed their time and expertise in numerous ways during the preparation of the final text.

Graphic production and copy-editing were expertly handled by Jacqueline Lalley. Tina Krumdick of KTK Design provided consultation on the design, which was a collaborative effort on the part of the FRC publications staff. The book was printed by Booklet Publishing Company.

Finally, *Guidelines for Family Support Practice* would not exist without the generous support of those who funded the Best Practices Project: Ongoing funding was provided by the A. L. Mailman Family Foundation and the Annie E. Casey Foundation, with additional funds for publication of commissioned papers contributed by The C. S. Mott Foundation, the Carnegie Corporation, and the Edna McConnell Clark Foundation. Funding from the Ford Foundation provided opportunities for the Latino and African American Caucuses of the Coalition to participate fully in the development of the book. The Evelyn and Walter Haas, Jr. Fund provided funds for dissemination of the book. The Johnson Foundation also provided funding. The U.S. Department of Health and Human Services provided funds to the Family Resource Coalition for the National Resource Center for Family Support Programs from 1991 to 1994 and for the National Resource Center for Family-Centered Practice beginning in 1995. These grants provided additional funding for staff time and research on the project.

We thank all of our funders for their continued support.

GUIDELINES FOR FAMILY SUPPORT PRACTICE

Families are responsible for the most important job in America: raising our next generation of learners, workers, and citizens. All of us will be affected by how well the families of today prepare their children for the future. What parents should do and how they should do it has been a topic for discussion as long as there have been parents and children. How our society at large should contribute to families' own efforts continues to be a subject of political debate. But while the debate goes on, families today are busy doing the best they can to see that their children are healthy and happy. And in neighborhoods and schools, in churches and homes, families are turning to a variety of resources for help.

The Need for Family Support

Throughout history, parents have used all kinds of support systems outside of their immediate families to help them raise their children. These systems have included networks of friends and neighbors; grandmothers and aunts who gave advice and care; religious organizations; sports teams and scouting organizations; and doctors, teachers, and other professionals who helped when they were needed. At this point in history, it is a fact of American life that these support systems are less available to all families than they used to be in every kind of community; while the challenges facing all parents and children, in every community, are greater than ever.

Today, times are tough for families. A number of economic factors from lack of job security to increasing numbers of mothers in the workforce have resulted in all families having less time and resources to devote to their children. Changes in family structure brought about by divorce, remarriage, and single parenthood have altered traditional bonds among family members. Geographic mobility has stranded young families far from the support of friends and members of their extended families. Many neighborhoods are not providing a safe, healthy environment for children. Growing poverty among children—in two-worker households as well as in single-parent households—has left many families without the means to meet basic needs.

The stress caused by such changes has left many adults less able to provide support to each other when it is needed most. These conditions for American families have resulted in children being increasingly at risk of ill health, impaired development, school failure, and homelessness; they also put children at greater risk of being both victims and future perpetrators of abuse, neglect, and violence. Parents know very well what they are up against, and they are struggling to do the best they can for their children. Seeking help in the difficult job of parenting is a sign of strength and intelligence, not a signal of weakness or failure.

The Family Support Response

The family support movement advocates a new national commitment to families. It began as an effort to combine knowledge about child development, family systems, and community impact on families in order to build more effective ways to promote healthy child development. It is a multicultural, multidisciplinary grassroots movement begun in the mid-1970s that represents thousands of community-based efforts dedicated to helping all kinds of families as they strive to raise healthy children. Family support is not intended to be only for "at-risk" families; it assumes that every family needs and deserves help, support, and access to resources.

Family support is an approach to working with families that assumes that all parents want to be "good parents" and will use whatever is available to help them achieve that goal. Many of the early programs that practiced this approach called themselves family *resource* programs to indicate their role as brokers of resources to families, to be used as families needed them and on families' own terms. The family support approach focuses on helping parents identify and develop their strengths, rather than relying on services designed and delivered by professional problem-solvers and received passively. Family support proponents consider parents who seek help to be active, involved, concerned directors of their families' lives and their children's development, not deficient and in need of being fixed.

1

What Do Family Support Programs Do?

Family support programs represent a national commitment to promoting healthy families and are designed to fill the gaps that families today are experiencing in their support systems. Family support programs share the goal of empowering and strengthening adults in their roles as parents, nurturers, and providers, but pursue that goal in diverse ways.

Many programs are comprehensive and provide a range of social, educational, and recreational activities; while others are designed to provide a single service, such as telephone support or parenting classes. Some programs serve specific populations, such as parents of teenagers and new parents. Others support families as they experience specific life events, such as teen pregnancy, divorce, family crisis, and relocation. Some are staffed by professionals, some by paraprofessionals, some by volunteers, and some by all three. Family support programs emerge under different auspices: some are private, nonprofit human service endeavors or other types of freestanding, fully independent programs; some are part of larger structures such as schools and hospitals.

Family support is intended to be a preventive measure that promotes healthy development of all families. Healthy family development can prevent child abuse and neglect, developmental delays in children, and crises that can lead to family break-up. Encouraging fathers—or mothers—who do not live with their children to be involved with them in a loving, appropriate way can also contribute significantly to the healthy development of both children and parents.

Family support programs can help families to make sense of the fragmented, categorical system of public services. In doing "whatever it takes" to support families, family support staff often act as service integrators, helping families navigate a maze of entitlements, appointments, and case managers.

There are five large categories of family support programs:

PROGRAMS THAT PROVIDE COMPREHENSIVE, COLLABORATIVE SERVICES

These large programs help families address many areas of need in their lives, including assistance with basic economic needs, housing, and job training as well as enhancing parenting skills. They often serve whole neighborhoods and are major stakeholders in community issues that affect families, including improvements in the social service delivery system.

PROGRAMS THAT ARE LINKED TO SCHOOL SUCCESS

Many school systems have sought to reach out to parents through family resource centers and other services designed to support parental involvement in their children's education. Non-school programs sometimes collaborate closely with schools to provide a range of family support opportunities at school sites or to offer home visiting programs to young parents before their children enter school.

PROGRAMS THAT SEEK TO ENHANCE PARENTING SKILLS AND FAMILY FUNCTIONING

These programs may be found in freestanding drop-in centers, seminars and workshops, or ongoing groups that meet in a variety of settings. Their purpose is specific: to build parents' skills and confidence in providing a nurturing environment for their children. Parents who use these programs come from a wide spectrum of backgrounds: from those who are concerned with providing the highest level of nurturing to their children to those who are mandated by court order to participate in parenting classes.

FAMILY SUPPORT AS A COMPONENT OF OTHER SERVICES

Family support sometimes is the "glue" that holds together a variety of services needed by families in certain situations or the approach through which other vital family services are provided. Substance abuse prevention, violence prevention, services to families of children with special needs, childcare, promotion of family literacy, and parent programs in the workplace fall into this category.

STATE FAMILY SUPPORT INITIATIVES

A number of states have begun statewide initiatives that are aimed at integrating different kinds of services for families or providing prevention services for certain targeted families and they typically include family support programs and services as a way to meet their goals. These initiatives usually have multiple sites, standardized program goals and outcome expectations, and staff trained in a common curriculum.

Some have extensive parent participation in local governance of programs.[1]

The Evolution of Family Support Programs

PROGRAM DEVELOPMENT

Family resource programs that began in the mid-1970s focused primarily on assisting parents in establishing a nurturing family environment in the earliest years of a child's life. A variety of excellent program models emerged during these years, and the practices they pioneered remain central to family support today. Some programs worked with teen parents to help them and their children to get off to the best start possible through mentoring and home visiting, health and educational services, and intensive parenting education. Other early programs supported middle-class parents who found themselves far away from extended family members or without a strong network of friends and neighbors to support them when their children were very young. All programs provided basic information about child development, activities for children and parents together, and links to other family services in the community. All programs fostered a welcoming environment so that parents could feel that in at least one place in their communities, someone understood and valued the work they were doing as parents.

The early programs developed in diverse settings in response to local needs. Programs that defined themselves as family support programs included freestanding local community organizations such as those funded by United Ways, religious institutions and organizations, parent groups that emerged from hospital-sponsored programs such as Lamaze, and groups of parents who banded together voluntarily for support as they struggled with establishing their families. Very few of these programs received any kind of government funding; primarily they relied on parent fundraising and donations from local individuals and foundations. Family resource programs that served teen parents or parents whose children had special needs sometimes received funding or staff from state or federal programs whose purpose was to serve these families.

A FAMILY SUPPORT APPROACH

In more recent years, many providers of programs and services for families—such as health and mental health care providers, childcare centers, and schools—began to adopt a more family-focused approach to their work. While these family-serving programs were not initiated as family support programs per se, they began to adapt and use principles of family support practice in their own programs. Both family support programs and programs that emerged from other disciplines benefited from an increasing exchange of ideas about the best ways to assist families.[2]

Parents of children with disabilities, for example, have long been involved in planning, overseeing, and evaluating the services that they and their children receive. Their experience in these areas has been used eagerly by family support programs that are committed to helping parents be effective advocates for themselves and their children. Community development programs and housing efforts have begun to utilize the expertise of local family support programs as child development and other services for children have taken a more prominent place on their agendas.

SYSTEMS REFORM

As state and large local governments have faced increasing problems in providing effective services for families, they have begun to look to family support ideas as a way to change their systems. State governments have come to view community-based programs as essential elements of an effective prevention agenda and of effective integration of services. As a result, funding for community-based programs has grown dramatically in the past ten years. A single program today may be receiving funds from JOBS and other self-sufficiency programs; the branches of its state or local government that administer services for maternal and child health, substance abuse prevention, child abuse prevention, mental health, and educational programs; foundations; and local fundraising. Programs may be in schools, health clinics, mental health care facilities, or housing developments.

In the past four years, federal funding for family support services has been provided to every state in the form of com-

3

prehensive child development programs, family support components of Head Start, the Family Preservation and Support Services Program, and the Community-Based Family Resource Program. In addition, virtually every state has initiated family resource centers of some kind; family support services for child abuse prevention; infant mortality reduction programs; and parent outreach programs in schools and in early childhood programs. State initiatives designed to make the welfare and job training systems serve families more comprehensively have also begun to use family support reasoning in their approaches. These are all indicators that traditional human services systems are beginning to adopt a family support approach to providing services and to reforming systems. It remains to be seen whether these systems will be able to fully integrate family support ideas into their way of working.

A NORMAL COMMUNITY RESPONSE

The family support movement's original vision of creating a new national response to families may be coming to fruition in local collaborations that are now emerging across the country. The original family support programs and other programs that have adopted a family support approach have long been an integral part of their communities' networks of support for families, often leading the way for parents to take leadership in efforts to improve the communities' support of families. The systems reform efforts, which are only at the beginning stages, have brought with them a new appreciation for the role of the community in determining how best to provide preventive resources for all families.

The authority to set priorities, to plan services, and to allocate resources for families that once lay with federal and state governments is reemerging at the local level with far greater participation among all stakeholders in the community, including parents. These new programs and services rely on mobilizing local resources to fill the many gaps left by categorical funding or funding based on eligibility standards. Sharing staff among agencies, relying on volunteers, being creative about finding space in which to provide services, and local fundraising are all elements of expanding and changing the way local communities support their families.

With new understanding of how both formal and informal resources should be stitched together to support families more effectively, local communities are at the forefront of making supportive resources for families a community priority: the normal way of doing business.

THE CONTEXT OF INCREASING DIVERSITY

One of the single greatest challenges facing our country today is finding ways to understand and draw strength from the increasing diversity among our families. While ethnic diversity is more pronounced in some regions of the country and large urban areas, it has an impact on the nation as a whole—and particular implications for those seeking to assist families in raising their children. According to the 1990 census, America's children and families are more racially, ethnically, and linguistically diverse than ever before. Between 1980 and 1990, the percentage of Latino, African American, Asian, and Native American children grew in every state in the nation. Approximately one-fourth of all children in the United States are from these groups. In a few states, such as Hawaii and California, such "minorities" now constitute a majority and there is no dominant ethnic group. In these two states, one out of seven children speaks a language other than English at home. Nationwide, one out of twenty-five children ages five to seventeen lives in a household in which all of the adults speak a language other than English and none speaks English well.[3]

Unfortunately, our society already bears the scars of past failures to promote the well-being of all of the groups that have made this country their home. During the last twenty years, the poverty rate of young families in the United States has almost doubled, and racial and ethnic minorities have fared the worst. African American, Native American, Latino, and Southeast Asian youngsters continue to drop out of school in higher proportions than those of other groups.[4] These are but a few of the troubling trends that reveal that ethnic minorities are still far from having adequate educational and economic opportunities. Family support programs cannot ignore the dramatic, accumulated impact of racism, poverty, and lack of power upon the lives of the families with

4

whom they work. Addressing these issues is a challenge that programs are working hard to address.

Premises of Family Support

In spite of the diversity of family support programs, virtually all programs share the same philosophical premises and underlying values. These values form the point of view from which family support programs have been initiated and developed and from which practice has emerged.

Primary responsibility for the development and well-being of children lies within the family, and all segments of society must support families as they rear their children.

The systems and institutions upon which families rely must effectively respond to their needs if families are to establish and maintain environments that promote growth and development. Achieving this requires a society that is committed to making the well-being of children and families a priority and to supporting that commitment by allocating and providing necessary resources.

Assuring the well-being of all families is the cornerstone of a healthy society, and requires universal access to support programs and services.

A national commitment to promoting the healthy development of families acknowledges that every family, regardless of race, ethnic background, or economic status, needs and deserves a support system. Since no family can be self-sufficient, the concept of reaching families before problems arise is not realized unless all families are reached. To do so requires a public mandate to make family support accessible and available, on a voluntary basis, to all.

Children and families exist as part of an ecological system.

An ecological approach assumes that child and family development is embedded within broader aspects of the environment, including a community with cultural, ethnic, and socio-economic characteristics that are affected by the values and policies of the larger society. This perspective assumes

that children and families are influenced by interactions with people, programs, and agencies as well as by values and policies that may help or hinder families' ability to promote their members' growth and development. The ecological context in which families operate is a critical consideration in programs' efforts to support families.

Child-rearing patterns are influenced by parents' understandings of child development and of their children's unique characteristics, personal sense of competence, and cultural and community traditions and mores.

There are multiple determinants of parents' child-rearing beliefs and practices, and each influence is connected to other influences. For example, a parent's view of her or his child's disposition is related to the parent's cultural background and knowledge of child development and to characteristics of the child. Since the early years set a foundation for the child's development, patterns of parent-child interaction are significant from the start. The unique history of the parent-child relationship is important to consider in programs' efforts.

Enabling families to build on their own strengths and capacities promotes the healthy development of children.

Family support programs promote the development of competencies and capacities that enable families and their members to have control over important aspects of their lives and to relate to their children more effectively. By building on strengths, rather than treating deficits, programs assist parents in dealing with difficult life circumstances as well as in achieving their goals, and in doing so, enhance parents' capacity to promote their children's healthy development.

The developmental processes that make up parenthood and family life create needs that are unique at each stage in the life span.

Parents grow and change in response to changing circumstances and to the challenges of nurturing a child's development. The tasks of parenthood and family life are ongoing and complex, requiring physical, emotional, and intellectual resources. Many tasks of parenting are unique to the needs of a child's developmental stage, others are unique to the parent's point in her or his life cycle. Parents have been influenced by their own childhood experiences and their own particular psychological characteristics, and are affected by their past and present family interactions.

Families are empowered when they have access to information and other resources and take action to improve the well-being of children, families, and communities.

Equitable access to resources in the community—including up-to-date information and high-quality services that address health, educational, and other basic needs—enables families to develop and foster optimal environments for all members. Meaningful experiences participating in programs and influencing policies strengthen existing capabilities and promote the development of new competencies in families, including the ability to advocate on their own behalf. (See appendix C for a copy of the premises of family support that is suitable for reproduction.)

Principles of Family Support Practice

Guidelines for Family Support Practice is built around principles that state how family support premises are carried out in family support programs. While specific practice strategies may be different in different program situations, they should all be consistent with the principles that guide family support work. After much discussion and input from thousands of people involved in family support programs, a consensus has emerged on the following principles to describe good family support practice:

1. Staff and families work together in relationships based on equality and respect.

2. Staff enhance families' capacity to support the growth and development of all family members—adults, youth, and children.

3. Families are resources to their own members, to other families, to programs, and to communities.

4. Programs affirm and strengthen families' cultural, racial, and linguistic identities and enhance their ability to function in a multicultural society.

5. Programs are embedded in their communities and contribute to the community-building process.

6. Programs advocate with families for services and systems that are fair, responsive, and accountable to the families served.

7. Practitioners work with families to mobilize formal and informal resources to support family development.

8. Programs are flexible and continually responsive to emerging family and community issues.

9. Principles of family support are modeled in all program activities, including planning, governance, and administration.

(See appendix C for a copy of the principles of family support practice that is suitable for reproduction.)

About this Book

How do the principles of family support guide the practice of community-based family support programs? What do family support programs need to do in order to operate according to the principles of family support? What constitutes quality practice in the field of family support?

These were the questions that prompted the investigation that was Family Resource Coalition's Best Practices Project. *Guidelines for Family Support Practice* is the culmination of that effort. In a very real sense, it is a compilation of the answers that programs in the field are providing to those questions. This book represents the state of the art in the field. Guidelines for family support practice have not been handed down from experts on high, but rather, they were gathered up from the real experts—practitioners working every day to strengthen and support families and to help families empower themselves.

In an effort to reduce redundancy and to offer a clear narrative, the principles have been clustered into themes, each of which describes a general area of practice. Each of these themes is covered in one of the practice chapters (chapters 2 through 6):

Chapter 2
Relationship Building (Principle 1)

Chapter 3
Enhancing Family Capacity (Principles 2 and 3)

Chapter 4
Affirming Diversity (Principle 4)

Chapter 5
Programs in Communities (Principles 5, 6, and 7)

Chapter 6
Program Planning, Governance, and Administration (Principles 8 and 9)

FORMAT OF CHAPTERS

Each of the chapters has the same format and contains three sections: an introductory overview, Guidelines for Practice, and Challenges in Practice.

Introduction

Each chapter begins with a shaded box that lists the principles covered in the chapter. This box is followed by a brief introductory essay that provides an overview of the theory and research underlying the principle(s) and related practices. The introduction to each chapter explains the chapter's rationale.

Guidelines for Practice

The bulk of each chapter is devoted to guidelines for operationalizing the principle(s) in practice. This section begins with an outline of the guidelines and key practices that programs should follow in order to realize the principle(s). For the purposes of this document, "guidelines" are practice goals. "Key practices" are the actions necessary to achieve the practice goals. The outline given at the beginning of the Guidelines for Practice section is annotated in subsequent pages, guideline by guideline, with the importance and value of each key practice. Programs use many different strategies for accomplishing the key practices. Examples of these strategies follow each key practice, and are separated by bullet

points. In the margins, large letters (corresponding to guidelines) and numbers (corresponding to key practices) help you know where you are in the outline (see Figure A).

Practice examples are dispersed throughout the Guidelines for Practice section of each chapter, in shaded boxes. These stories illustrate some of the key practices and strategies described in the chapter; many also show how the principles work together. Although these stories are based on the actual experiences of families and practitioners in local programs (and are sometimes verbatim testimonials), names, program locations, and other identifying characteristics have been changed to preserve anonymity. All program names are fictitious; any correspondence to an existing program is entirely coincidental. The decision to avoid specifically locating practice examples was made in order to emphasize that it is not the experience of a specific person or the practice of a specific program that should be the focus of attention and analysis, but rather the lessons to be learned by applying the guidelines, key practices, and strategies to real-life situations.

There is some unavoidable overlap of practices described in the different chapters. The interdependence of the principles makes it impossible to completely eliminate discussion of some practices in more than one chapter, because whereas each of the principles represents a separate, vital element of family support, many practices are integral to more than one principle. (For example, gathering input from participants and involving them in program decisions is a necessary part of operationalizing almost every principle.) Cross-references that refer the reader to other chapters have been employed to reduce overlap and to minimize redundancy.

Challenges in Practice

The last section of each chapter describes challenges that programs often encounter when they attempt to operate in accordance with the family support principle(s) described in that chapter. Suggestions for meeting these challenges and for overcoming barriers to quality practice in accordance with family support principles are offered.

The book's concluding chapter, "Looking to the Future," discusses how guidelines for family support can inform practice, training and education of family support workers, research and evaluation, and public policy. Following that chapter are a list of recommended resources and an appendix that describes the process of which this book is an outcome.

NOTES

[1] For additional information on types of family support programs, see the following books published by the Family Resource Coalition: *Programs to Strengthen Families* (1992), *The Basics of Family Support: A Guide for State Planners (and Others)* (1994), and *From Communities to Capitols: State Experiences With Family Support* (1996). Also see *Raising Our Future: Families, Schools, and Communities Joining Together* (1995) (Cambridge, Mass.: Harvard Family Research Project).

[2] For a review of literature on the effects of family support programs, see Powell, D. R. (1994) "Evaluating family support programs: Are we making progress?" In S. L. Kagan and B. Weissbourd, eds., *Putting families first: America's family support movement and the challenge of change.* (1994) (San Francisco, Calif.: Jossey-Bass) 441–470.

[3] *The challenge of change: What the 1990 census tells us about children.* (1992) (Washington, D.C.: Center for the Study of Social Policy).

[4] *Digest of education statistics.* (1995) (Washington, D.C.: Department of Education).

Principle One
Staff and families work together in relationships based on equality and respect.

Relationship building is the heart of family support practice, and is therefore the first theme discussed in *Guidelines for Family Support Practice*. An effective, empowering relationship between families and the family resource program staff member is the essential foundation on which all other elements of family support practice are built. Establishing a true partnership between families and staff takes time, skill, and commitment on the part of practitioners and extensive support from programs. It is important for all program staff and sponsors to understand why a particular kind of relationship between families and practitioners has emerged as the cornerstone of family support.

Parent and Staff Roles in Respectful, Egalitarian Partnerships

The family support movement defines the optimal relationship between families and family support programs as a partnership that requires the expertise and active participation of each partner. Parents' experience and information regarding their own families are just as important as the more general expertise that professionals bring. Families are considered to be the final decision makers about their own priorities and needs; family support professionals contribute appropriate resources, insight, and information to the situation at hand. At the same time, acknowledging the family's right to self-determination does not relieve the professional from responsibility for ensuring the physical and emotional safety of family members if they are in danger.

The practitioner's primary roles in the relationship are (1) to be a trustworthy, dependable advocate who provides practical as well as emotional support; (2) to offer specific knowledge and skill about healthy child development and how parents can support it; (3) to facilitate families' ongoing access to information and resources that they need; (4) to enable parents to develop the skills that they need in order to be advocates for themselves and their families; and (5) to provide avenues for families to contribute to the life and development of their community.

Parents' roles in the partnership are (1) to be the primary resources that contribute to their children's healthy development; (2) to act as advocates and agents of change on behalf of themselves and their families; (3) to share information about their families, including their values and beliefs, with practitioners; and (4) to take responsibility for their ongoing participation in their partnership with staff.

Staff roles vary from situation to situation. For example, in a program that provides parents with basic child development information, staff may meet parents' needs by acting as "experts"; by helping parents learn from other parents; and, of course, by being supportive, empathic listeners. In a program that serves families who are under inordinate stress and are coping with multiple challenges, staff may also act as "case managers," supporting parents as they utilize a succession of services and resources. For families who are enrolled in workshops or classes, staff may serve as teachers who emphasize interactive learning relationships with parents.

The context of the program sets some parameters for staff roles. In a program whose contact with families is primarily through home visiting, the home visitor plays roles that run the whole gamut of possibilities. In a program whose primary vehicle for serving families is a drop-in center, staff assume a variety of roles and have a different relationship with each family who participates.

The needs that each family expresses also determine the roles that the practitioner assumes. Families in crisis will need immediate, emergency direction and concrete responses to their crises. Mothers who attend a program to relieve their loneliness and find a network of friends may not be looking for an intensive relationship with a staff member. Families struggling with poverty may want an advocate who is results-oriented and realistic, and who will help them move toward economic security. In each case, staff respond to families by treating them as the chief decision makers regarding their

9

needs and desires, and by fulfilling their own role as valuable resources and providers of support for families.

The family support approach of egalitarian relationships between practitioners and families stands in contrast to a model of helping in which the professional is dominant. In this model, the professional is the "helper," and is endowed with expertise and authority that the family—the party to be "helped"—does not have. By virtue of his or her expertise, the professional is empowered to name the problems that are to be fixed, decide the family's priorities, and choose the best course of action for correcting a problem. In this context, families' experience of the helping relationship may be that it compounds their sense of impotence to control their own lives, rather than actually helping them move toward their goals. Family support practice intends to replace this model with one that encourages families to actively participate in their relationships with program staff.

Family support programs are intended to be universal, that is, open to all families in a community. On one hand, this policy sends a strong message that all families need and deserve assistance in the important job of parenting. Family support is not intended to be only for families who are "at risk" or facing some kind of crisis. It is available for families to use on a voluntary basis when they need it, on their own schedule and on their own terms.

On the other hand, universality means that family support programs serve families who are mandated by court order to participate in parenting classes or other services offered by the family support program. To carry out its promise to serve all families, a family support program serves families who are in crisis or in danger of having their parental rights challenged due to child abuse or neglect as well as families who participate of their own volition. In these cases, staff take a respectful approach to families and honor the importance of establishing a workable partnership between staff and family, just as they do in all other cases. Practitioners recognize that while attending a family support program can be mandated, participation that is collaborative, engaged, and enthusiastic is always voluntarily contributed.

Why Relationship Building Is Critical

The overall goal of family support programs is the healthy development of children; programs' approach to achieving this goal is to encourage and support parents so that they can provide optimal nurturing environments for their children. While there are many different strategies for supporting parents, all of them depend heavily on (1) parents' ongoing commitment to receiving support and to examining their own child-rearing practices and (2) practitioners' understanding and responsiveness to families' issues. By underscoring the self-determination of families, respectful relationships between staff and families enhance parents' motivation to provide what their children need in order to develop optimally.

When families define their own needs, they are likely to be invested in working to address them. They become empowered to take action on their own behalf, and become more confident that they have the capacity to grow. Long-standing evidence indicates that individuals who are in control of defining and addressing their own needs experience both enhanced capacity and enhanced belief in their own ability.[1]

Programs that take an empowerment approach[2] to serving families report that families experience increased self-esteem and self-confidence, in addition to developing skills and knowledge that they can use in many settings.[3] Staff of these programs create many opportunities for parents to make decisions, set their own agendas, and take action. The programs yield more consistent results for families than those that do not take an empowerment approach.[4] A number of studies have shown that it is important that the services offered to families match families' own perceptions of their own needs and interests. Help that is not wanted by the family or that is inconsistent with the needs, problems, and goals that they have identified for themselves has been shown to reduce the family's investment in participating.[5]

A respectful relationship with a family support practitioner can be a powerful antidote to the abandonment, ridicule, and devaluation that parents may have experienced in previous attempts to secure needed resources. Families struggling to get what they need to survive often find it difficult to hang on to their self-esteem and to have confidence in their own ability to create change. Their experience may be that almost everything in their environment, including relationships with other people, has been a barrier to fulfilling their goals. A practitioner who consistently does not give up on a family, even if parents miss appointments or initially refuse to open their door for a home visit, can help the family understand that the relationship will not lead to further rejection.[6]

For families in ethnic, racial, or linguistic minority groups, supportive relationships with family support staff who validate and promote their cultural values and practices can create opportunities to develop new strengths and to set and reach goals.[7] These families may be overwhelmed by barriers to opportunities and resources, and may have experienced the devaluation of their history, values, norms, language, and style of interaction by the dominant culture.[8] A practitioner who consistently conveys the message that participants are welcomed and respected, and that the program will work alongside the family to ameliorate the devaluing effects of discrimination, offers the family a strong incentive to mobilize their own resources and those of the community and program to accomplish their own goals.[9]

Finally, relationship building is important because parents say so. Parents report that caring relationships with staff are the key factor in their continued involvement with a program. It is "the heart and soul of services, ... not information, instruction, or procedures" that seem to make the most difference for families.[10] Parents feel most positive about their relationships with practitioners when they feel a sense of control over the process of meeting their own goals. Parents call for practitioners to value their role as partners, and as final arbitrators on behalf of their own children.[11] Families across the nation participated in focus groups to help determine these guidelines for practice in family support; they too, said that relationships based on equality and respect made all the difference in the world to them.

NOTES

[1] Bandura, A. (1982) "Self-efficacy mechanism in human agency." *American Psychologist* 37 (2) 122–147.

Rappaport, J. (1984) "Studies in empowerment: Introduction to the issues." In J. Rappaport, C. Swift, and R. Hess, eds., *Studies in empowerment: Steps toward understanding and action.* (New York: Haworth Press) 1–7.

[2] Empowerment is defined by the Cornell Empowerment Group as: an intentional, ongoing process centered in the local community involving mutual respect, critical reflection, caring, and group participation, through which people lacking an equal share of valued resources gain greater access to and control over those resources.

[3] Cochran, M., (1995) "Empowerment through family support". In M.Cochran, ed., *Empowerment and family support* 1(1). (Ithaca, New York: Cornell Media Services) 2.

[4] Massinga, R. (1994) "Transforming social services: Family supportive strategies." In S. L. Kagan and B. Weissbourd, eds., *Putting families first: America's Family Support Movement and the Challenge of Change.* (San Francisco, Calif.: Jossey-Bass) 93–111.

[5] Fisher, J. D. (1983) "Recipient reactions to aid: The parameters of the field." In J.D. Fisher, A. Nadler, and B.M. DePaulo, eds., *New directions in helping: Volume 1, Recipient reactions to aid.* (New York: Academic Press) 3–14.

[6] Pawl, J. and A. F. Lieberman (1993) "Infant-parent psychotherapy." In C. Zeanah, ed., *Handbook for infant mental health.* (New York: Guilford Press) 427–442.

[7] Norton, D. (1990) "Understanding early experiences of black children in high risk environments: Culturally and ecologically relevant research as a guide to support families." *Zero to Three 10* (4) 1–8.

[8] Baca-Zinn, M. (1994) "Changing the way scholars think about Latino families." *FRC Report 13* (3–4) 15–18.

[9] Pinderhughes, E. (1989)*Understanding race, ethnicity and power: The key to efficacy in clinical practice.* (New York: Free Press).

[10] Larner, M., R. Halpern, and O. Harkavy (1992) *Fair start for children: Lessons learned from seven demonstration projects.* (New Haven, Conn.: Yale University Press) 248. In same source, see also Halpern, R., "Issues of program design and implementation" (179–197).

[11] Pizzo, P. (1987) "Parent to parent support groups: Advocates for social change." In S. L. Kagan , D. R. Powell, B. Weissbourd, and E. Zigler, eds., *America's family support programs: Perspectives and prospects.* (New Haven, Conn.:Yale University Press) 228–242.

Relationship Building: Guidelines for Practice

Relationship building is a dynamic and ongoing process that begins with a family's first encounter with the program and with a staff member's first day on the job. Building and maintaining relationships based on equality and respect takes effort and time. It is a process of continually seeking to understand assumptions and to share meanings and expectations. It requires a mutual recognition of the roles each partner plays and a realization that these roles change over time. This section will detail the specific practices necessary to establish and maintain family-supportive partnerships based on equality and respect.

Guidelines and Key Practices

Guideline A: Programs create a family-friendly environment.
Key Practices
1. Provide a welcoming, non-stigmatizing atmosphere.
2. Hire staff members who are from the community or who have extensive knowledge of the community's demographics and experiences.
3. Structure activities with families' schedules and time commitments in mind.
4. Create opportunities for informal dialogue among parents and staff.

Guideline B: Family support practitioners seek to understand family members' values and perspectives.
Key Practices
1. Strive to learn the priorities, beliefs, and expectations about relationships held by family members.
2. Recognize that it takes time to get to know a family.

Guideline C: Family support practitioners and families develop collaborative partnerships.
Key Practices
1. Respect the resources, rights, and responsibilities that each partner brings to the relationship.
2. Create many opportunities for formal and informal feedback from participants—and act on that feedback.
3. Create opportunities for families and staff to share leadership.
4. Enable families to contribute their time and skills to the program.

Guideline D: Family support practitioners demonstrate positive, responsive caring toward the families with whom they work.
Key Practices
1. Demonstrate genuine interest in and concern for families.
2. Validate and support the cultural identity and development of each family.
3. Celebrate and appreciate program participants.
4. Face difficult issues with families at their own pace and on their own terms.
5. Persevere.

Guideline E: Family support practitioners communicate responsibly and effectively with families.
Key Practices
1. Listen empathically and pay attention to the way family members respond to what you say.
2. Balance supportive, accepting interaction with open, honest communication about disagreements.

Guideline A: Programs create a family-friendly environment.

Key Practice 1: Provide a welcoming, non-stigmatizing atmosphere.

The environment of every program, no matter what type, sends a message to parents from the moment they walk in. Providing a warm, friendly atmosphere through physical surroundings and human interaction is the first step in building a relationship. Family support programs strive to create a comfortable place in which all families feel relaxed, at ease, and welcome. Respect for families is conveyed when it is obvious that care has been given to making the surroundings attractive.

Some ways to accomplish this are:

● Creating a home-like, rather than institutional, atmosphere. Programs do this by emphasizing family space over office space and by furnishing and decorating the center to be inviting, casual, and relaxing. Programs make sure that furnishings, whether new or old, are clean and well maintained.

● Providing comfortable, informal seating space with food and hot or cold drinks for adults. This area can be adjacent to a children's play area. Many programs pay particular attention to the children's play area, ensuring that it is a rich environment with many objects and toys, including manipulatives, and planned activities such as storytelling.

● Greeting families warmly when they arrive at the program. Some programs designate a staff member or a parent volunteer to be a greeter.

● Involving participants in deciding how space will be used. Most programs discuss with participants how program space will be used, even down to what type of information will be placed on bulletin boards. Programs with ample space have created lounges with TVs, VCRs, comfortable chairs, and reading materials in response to participants' requests. Others have set aside space for needed community resources, such as laundry facilities.

● Decorating the program in a way that reflects the cultural and socio-economic life of participants. Many programs decorate their walls with community-appropriate posters or photographs of participants engaging in program activities. Others display crafts or art work done by program participants.

Key Practice 2: Hire staff members who are from the community or who have extensive knowledge of the community's demographics and experiences.

Families are comfortable walking into a program when they are met by staff members with whom they can identify. For this reason, many programs are staffed at all levels with people who represent the race, ethnicity, and socio-economic background of the participants. It can be a source of pride to participants when staff members in leadership positions represent their culture. Though it is not necessary that all staff members be of the same origin as the population served by the program, all must be knowledgeable about and sensitive to the culture, values, practices, history, and language of the families who participate. The objective is for families to find staff members in the program whom they trust and to whom they can relate.

Some ways for programs to accomplish this are:

- Hiring bilingual or bicultural staff members. In programs where many of the participants are of a particular cultural background, or speak a language other than English, programs hire staff members who speak that language and come from that culture. Many programs have found that it is important to be aware of diversity within cultures and to pay attention to specific cultural background when recruiting staff members. For example, a program in a Mexican American neighborhood would recruit Spanish-speaking staff people, but would want to be aware that a Puerto Rican staff person's culture and life experience might be very different from those of families in the community, and would want to be sure that the staff person understood the Mexican community. In any case, it is essential that staff members who are not of the culture understand the culture.

Practice Example

When Mr. and Mrs. Wu saw the invitation to attend an open house of the Chinatown Family Resource Center in their church bulletin, they decided to attend out of curiosity. Since coming to this country nine months earlier, they'd been so busy setting up their new home, finding jobs, and figuring out where to find all that they needed that they hadn't had much time or opportunity to meet other people in the community. Upon their arrival at the open house, they found themselves among many other Chinese families, some of whom they recognized from the neighborhood and others whom they did not know. Families chatted in familiar dialects over homemade *dim sum*.

Soon afterward, the mostly–Chinese-speaking staff began to introduce themselves. Most were first-generation immigrants, as were many of the families in attendance. Staff also informed the group about the center's mission: to provide support to the Chinese community, including help understanding U.S. systems.

After the introductions and overview, families broke into small, informal groups, just to talk. There were two Cantonese-speaking groups, one Mandarin-speaking group, and one Tiao Chew–speaking group. Mr. and Mrs. Wu gathered with a group of other Cantonese speakers; some, like them, were ethnic Chinese from Viet Nam. The group was facilitated by a family resource worker who was fluent in English and Cantonese. The worker answered families' questions about what activities went on at the center and asked them what activities they'd find helpful. Mrs. Wu decided that she should come back on Thursday evening after work when a volunteer lawyer would be available to answer questions on immigration.

- Recruiting program participants or other community members to join the staff. Programs hire staff members whose backgrounds, life experiences, and challenges have been similar to those of program participants, either as full-time staff members or to fulfill specific roles with respect to specific program components. Programs hire men to provide outreach and resources to fathers and other male family members, younger staff to address the particular concerns and interests of young parents, and elder family members to work with parenting grandparents.

- Assessing the attitude of potential staff members as part of the hiring process. Regardless of race or ethnicity, programs hire as staff members people who are open to learning about other cultures, who are respectful of differences, and who are clearly compassionate and sensitive to the needs of families in the community.

- Providing training and staff development opportunities on cultural competence. Some programs include this as part of regular staff meetings; others have periodic workshops that are facilitated by trained and experienced consultants. All programs recognize that learning about cultures is an ongoing process that first and foremost requires dialogue and willingness to learn.

- Establishing ways for parents and community residents to take part in staff recruitment and selection.

3

Key Practice 3: Structure activities with families' schedules and time commitments in mind.

Central to building relationships of respect is giving consideration to and honoring families' schedules and time commitments. When staff members are interested in knowing what families' constraints are, programs convey the message that families' needs are important. Families appreciate being consulted about the timing of program activities. They are more likely to participate if staff members set the program schedule with their needs in mind.

Some ways for programs to accomplish this are:

● Making staff hours flexible. Programs are open and available to families outside of nine-to-five working hours; many provide services in the evening and on weekends.

● Consulting family members when scheduling activities. Staff members talk to families about possible times for activities. They make appointments with families in a way that respects family members' schedules and the demands on their time. Many programs offer services, classes, and workshops after working hours or on weekends.

● Providing time-saving respite for parents. Many programs offer childcare, transportation, or meals served at the times of scheduled activities to make it easier for family members to attend.

● Encouraging feedback and criticism, including scheduling time for discussing problems and how to address them. Programs often provide time and space for parents to meet without program staff to discuss their perspectives and to decide and plan how to present to staff any concerns they have.

Practice Example

Every day around 11:30 a.m., the smell of rice, beans, and other delicacies drifts throughout the two-story townhouse that is home to the family resource center in a primarily Latino, urban neighborhood. Most of the participants in the program are women who are newly arrived immigrants from Central America and whose families are supported by low-paying service jobs, often with evening or irregular hours. Most residents of the neighborhood are grateful for opportunities to stretch their already-tight food budgets, so every day the center provides a communal hot lunch for anyone who comes through its doors at noon. Program participants sign up in advance to volunteer to cook. They take over the kitchen and prepare whatever donated food is on hand to feed themselves, their children, the center's staff, and their neighbors. Children safely play in the center's childcare room.

Much more than recipes are shared over the hot skillets, chopping blocks, and boiling pots. Child-rearing advice is shared. Neighborhood gossip is traded. Friendships are made.

4

Key Practice 4: Create opportunities for informal dialogue among parents and staff.

In order to build strong relationships, people must talk to each other and get to know each other's hopes, fears, and ways of viewing the world. Effective family resource programs recognize the importance of informal dialogue and create opportunities for practitioners and families to exchange ideas, reflections on their experiences, and information.

Some ways for programs to accomplish this are:

● Offering program activities that are designed to bring families together. Some programs offer drop-in hours. Others plan play groups for parents and children. Events such as family picnics, special dinners, regular potlucks, and holiday celebrations help participants develop a sense of community.

● Providing opportunities for informal discussion before, during, and/or after planned activities.

B

1

2

Guideline B: Family support practitioners seek to understand family members' values and perspectives.

Key Practice 1: Strive to learn the priorities, beliefs, and expectations about relationships held by family members.

Values, beliefs, and expectations about relationships vary widely among individuals, families, and cultures, as do experiences with attempts to obtain needed resources and support. For example, some family members enter a program confident about their ability to build relationships with staff members and other parents. Others enter with great distrust. A family member whose culture or family has placed a high value on independence or who has been taught that seeking help is a sign of weakness might feel embarrassed or ashamed about participating in a family resource program. Those who have had experiences with social services agencies that left them feeling disrespected and disempowered might be fearful or hostile. Understanding these factors with respect to a specific family encourages communication, strengthens the bond between family and practitioner, and enhances family members' feeling of being respected.

Some ways to accomplish this are:

● Talking to family members about their experiences seeking support and resources. Staff ask parents if they have ever participated in a family support program before. If so, they ask what their experience with that program was, what they liked and what they didn't like. Have they ever obtained other kinds of services for their family from private or public agencies? If so, what happened? Staff also discuss with families what they expect and would like from the program.

● Considering things from family members' points of view. Practitioners ask questions and listen to family members in order to obtain a full understanding of what they are experiencing as the relationship develops. Practitioners use this information to begin identifying and addressing any barriers to relationship building. They consider environment, life situations, and other factors when making judgments.

● Soliciting input from and comparing perceptions with other staff members. Some programs devote a portion of staff meetings to such discussions. Others structure staff members' roles and time to promote staff-to-staff consultation. Programs are careful to stress that such discussions about families should occur in private and should always remain confidential.

Key Practice 2: Recognize that it takes time to get to know a family.

Family support practitioners understand that learning a family's strengths, needs, and goals comes from building a relationship over a long period of time. In order for families to reveal personal information, especially issues that are difficult or painful to talk about, they must trust the person to whom they are speaking. Building trust is an ongoing process that develops with every interaction between family members and practitioners. Program policies can facilitate this process.

Some ways for programs to accomplish this are:

● Making sure that staff are able to devote the time and energy necessary to learn about each family's concerns and resources. This is especially important when the program offers intensive one-on-one work with families, such as home visiting or individual counseling.

● Structuring program activities to allow time for practitioners and families to get to know one another. Many programs are drop-in programs or schedule drop-in hours when families and staff can talk informally. Other programs provide flexible, open-ended classes in which participants can discuss their own issues. Programs offer activities which involve staff and families as groups but also allow interaction between staff and families on an individual basis, such as family potlucks or mom-and-tot events.

● Allowing for private time between staff and families. Some programs offer home visits or family or individual counseling. In programs without formal components that allow this private time, staff members create the time and space informally and spontaneously: for example, a staff member and a parent may go to a corner of a room or to the staff person's office to talk privately.

● Ensuring that staff have flexibility within their schedules to respond to unanticipated opportunities with families. Families will recognize that it is not always possible for staff to drop what they are doing to respond to them, but providing staff with flexibility in managing their time can facilitate staff being available at those times when families are particularly receptive or eager to open up and share.

Guideline C: Family support practitioners and families develop collaborative partnerships.

Key Practice 1: Respect the resources, rights, and responsibilities that each partner brings to the relationship.
Family support practitioners bring to their interactions with families knowledge and expertise about child development and family functioning, as well as knowledge about and access to resources needed by families. Families bring specialized knowledge about their children, their own dynamics and history, what has worked and not worked for them over time, and the cultural and socio-economic realities of their communities. It is the right of parents to advocate for their families' needs and desires, and it is the right of practitioners to uphold reasonable professional and program standards. Both partners are responsible for maintaining a healthy, productive relationship between each other and with the program. Understanding and respecting each other's resources, rights, and responsibilities strengthens the partnership.

Some ways to accomplish this are:

● Sharing information freely with families. Practitioners fully inform families about the policies and rules which have an impact on their relationship with the program, and openly discuss with families their professional responsibility and reporting requirements. For example, families are informed from the beginning of their involvement in the program about the conditions that would require a staff member to file a child abuse report. Families are made aware of their right to expect confidentiality about what they share with program staff, and they can easily observe that practitioners do not talk about families to representatives of other agencies without the parents' knowledge.

● Ensuring that family members' voices and priorities are taken seriously in the program and by other service providers. Program staff are advocates for families in internal program planning meetings as well as in their work with other community agencies.

● Filling out necessary paperwork with families present and participating. Practitioners use family members' own words when filling out forms, then carefully review what has been written with family members. Practitioners gain family members' permission to reveal information before anything is written.

● Treating parents as experts. Program staff recognize, involve, and consult family members in all facets of program activity. Staff consciously model respect for families whenever they are around representatives from other programs and agencies.

Key Practice 2: Create many opportunities for formal and informal feedback from participants—and act on that feedback.

Feedback from participants allows staff to maintain a program responsive to families' needs and desires. Families feel equal to and respected by practitioners when it is clear that their opinions and judgments—particularly those that concern the services which they are receiving—are viewed as important and taken seriously. Eliciting feedback and acting on participants' recommendations enhances program effectiveness and communicates respect.

Some ways to accomplish this are:

● Creating a climate that encourages communication. Programs do this by having regular open meetings and informal conversations with family members, encouraging phone conversations, producing newsletters, or creating notebooks of messages that travel between staff and parents.

● Setting up and using formal feedback and evaluation channels. Some programs conduct focus groups and interviews. Others use participant satisfaction surveys and evaluation questionnaires.

● Convening participant-led group discussions about program practices. Programs may schedule special feedback sessions for reflection, assessment, and changes in plans.

● Gathering feedback from a range of families and family types. It is important to receive input from families who

2

Practice Example

When our second daughter turned two last fall, my wife, Peggy, and I reevaluated the household situation: Peggy had put her career on hold to be with the kids full time. She was eager to get back to work as a hospital administrator, and she had a friend who knew of an opening in the hospital where she worked. The company where I work in database management was cutting back in my division and offered me the option to go part-time. I took it.

As exhausting as it can be, I love being home with my kids and being a part of all of their everyday victories and changes. Going grocery shopping is one of our favorite activities. Since most of my contacts are through my work, I look forward to shopping as a way to make contact with people in the neighborhood.

A couple of months ago I noticed a small sign in the doorway leading to the grocery store: Volunteer Needed For Computer Database Project. The family resource center wanted someone to design and implement a database of community resources: skills such as cooking, auto repair, athletic coaching, as well as material resources such as large rooms for activities or even clothing and books. That sign might as well have had my name on it.

I've been using some of my time at home during the day to create a database that can keep track of all these resources. As I've been looking through the cards that people have filled out, I've found that our community has a lot more to offer than I'd ever guessed. I'm going to get more involved in the center, and I hope this database is something that I can help expand and maintain.

are reserved or cautious as well as from those who are always available and forthcoming with opinions and information, and from families who are pressed for time and resources as well as those under less pressure.

- Keeping the focus on parents' concerns and input. Staff members see themselves as parent advocates, making sure that parents' opinions and requests are always taken seriously and treated with respect.

Key Practice 3: Create opportunities for families and staff to share leadership.

Programs model partnership by sponsoring activities in which staff members and families work together as equal partners, and by encouraging parents to take the lead on these activities often. These opportunities reinforce families' contributions to the program and build relationships between and among program staff and families. They contribute to empowering families and to building parents' confidence and competence.

Some ways to accomplish this are:

- Having parents provide in-service training for staff members. For example, parents may provide a workshop for staff on outreach methods and suggested ways to talk about family support and the program to community residents.

- Working on projects together. Programs convene committees of program participants and staff members to plan and implement activities and projects. These may include any number of activities, such as parenting classes and support groups, special events such as birthday parties and holiday celebrations, fundraisers, planting a community garden, or organizing an advocacy campaign.

- Involving and utilizing the special skills of staff and families in all aspects of the program. Programs include parents in their governance structure. Parents may provide life skills classes or workshops for other parents (for example in sewing or bookkeeping) or may volunteer their talents to the program.

Practice Example

When our son was born with spina bifida and other problems, we thought the world was going to end. Sometimes I thought we were going to lose him. Other times I thought about what kind of future we might have with him, and then I wished he wouldn't make it. Instead of being filled with love and joy for my newborn, as I imagined I would be during my pregnancy, I found myself struggling to love him. Then I just felt guilty about and ashamed of my feelings.

We met Marta, a family support worker, while I was still in the hospital. The first time she came to our house, we talked for close to two hours. I knew she understood about the roller coaster of emotions that my husband and I were experiencing. At one point, she asked if she could hold the baby, and she warmly smiled and talked to him.

Marta arranged for us to meet another couple that had a two-year-old with spina bifida, and our two families have become fast friends. It has helped to see how they manage to be a caring, loving family despite the hardships. Marta and our new friends have told us to call anytime—day or night—whenever depression or despair sets in, and we do. I've started having hope that we too will be capable of loving and raising our special child.

Key Practice 4: Enable families to contribute their time and skills to the program.

When parents and practitioners are engaged in a collaborative partnership, parents know their value and the importance of their contributions to the program. Sending a clear message that the program is enhanced by the particular skills parents bring encourages parents to share their abilities and talents. Recognizing families' assets and asking them to use these strengths and skills in ways that contribute to the program's and the community's well-being is a form of respect, and it helps to broaden the capacity of the program. In addition, many programs have found that families who benefit from a program's services often want to "give something back" to the program. Respecting that desire and creating opportunities for families to contribute reinforces the collaborative partnership between families and practitioners. Families should have opportunities to reciprocate by assisting other families or making contributions to the program as a whole. These opportunities should be in response to participants' expressed desire to reciprocate; families should not feel pressured or obligated to volunteer their time and effort at times or in ways that are uncomfortable for them.

Some ways for programs to accomplish this are:

● Establishing a barter system within the program. Some programs assign services or resources contributed by parents a measurable value that families can trade for other services they need. One family may have three hours of credit in their "account," gained by assisting with childcare at the program. They can use this credit to get an hour of assistance in filling out tax returns, offered by another parent in the program. Other programs offer direct exchange boards or directories in which families can list offers to barter services—for example, a family will offer childcare in exchange for tutoring for one of its children.

● Encouraging families to donate concrete resources. Some programs encourage families to cook meals for families in need, if they are able to. Others have food or clothing pantries, thrift shops, or toy or book libraries to which families can contribute and from which they can draw.

● Creating opportunities for family members to volunteer in program activities. Some programs train participants as volunteer outreach workers, home visitors, or information providers. Others encourage parents to lead support groups or to offer classes that utilize their special skills—for example, in computer use, cooking, sewing, gardening, or arts and crafts—to other interested parents.

Guideline D: Family support practitioners demonstrate positive, responsive caring toward the families with whom they work.

Key Practice 1: Demonstrate genuine interest in and concern for families.
Most people can see through a facade of concern; genuineness builds trust and enhances respect. A receptive attitude conveys to family members that they are valued and respected. Over time, as family members come to know that the practitioner is interested in and concerned about them and will not negatively judge them, ridicule them, or look down on them, the family-practitioner partnership will grow. The program contributes to this practice by staffing the program with people who relate to families in a positive way, recruiting and hiring only staff who exhibit a natural tendency to relate well to families, and providing training and support for staff to strengthen this natural tendency.

Some ways to accomplish this are:

● Expressing interest in families. Staff members consciously and consistently ask about the well-being of family members and listen and inquire when family members share new ideas and experiences. They stop to greet families who are waiting in a common area. They treat phone calls from parents as important. Practitioners spend time with and pay attention to children while their parents are present.

● Being available when families are having difficulties. Many programs have flexible hours and drop-in times. Some programs also make it possible for families to reach staff when the program is not in session by having staff members carry beepers, establishing a twenty-four-hour hotline or warm-line, authorizing staff members to give families their home phone numbers, or having twenty-four-hour voice mail that staff check periodically.

● Speaking respectfully about families. Programs urge staff to pay attention to the way they speak with and about families in informal settings (both with each other and with other families) and in formal settings, such as staff meetings. Family support practitioners refer to families as participants, parents, or partners rather than clients, cases, referrals, or other terms that create distance between program staff and family members.

Key Practice 2: Validate and support the cultural identity and development of each family.

Building a relationship of trust with families requires an understanding and authentic validation of their cultural identities. Validation includes recognizing the potential impact of devaluation and discrimination that families of different ethnic or racial groups may encounter. Understanding the richness that culture contributes to an individual's identity as well as the costs of being different in this society enables a practitioner to relate to families in ways that make them feel respected, supported, and validated. (See chapter 4.)

Some ways to accomplish this are:

● Learning about other cultures. Practitioners find that their cultural competence is enhanced by reading widely about cultures different from their own (including fiction), talking with people of other cultures about their cultures, and talking with people about discrimination that they have encountered.

● Creating formal and informal opportunities for cultural exchange and celebration. Programs host social events and holiday celebrations, sponsor artistic displays and performances, publish newsletters and other publications, and show movies and videos.

Practice Example

A family resource center, located in one of the larger urban areas in an otherwise rural state and near a Native American Indian reservation, serves a predominately Sioux population. Pregnancy and parenthood among teenagers are common in this community. There is a severe shortage of affordable, safe housing, and a lack of transportation.

It is forty-five minutes before the teen parenting discussion group begins at the family resource center and Sara, the family resource worker who facilitates the group, starts out for her biweekly rounds to pick up participants. Sometimes it takes two or three stops for Sara to find the mother and baby she has set out to find.

"So many of these girls need to leave their homes when they become pregnant, but there's nowhere for them to go," Sara explains. "For many different reasons they often end up piecing together various living arrangements. They stay some nights with one friend or relative, others with their boyfriend, and so on. I know all their regular places. It may take a while, but I find them!"

Soon Sara's Delta 88 is filled with two moms and their three youngsters. "I don't have a car and I don't have a place of my own, so I usually stay with friends," says one of the moms. "Most days, this is the only time I get out, and I wouldn't be able to come if Sara didn't come get me."

Sara makes three different runs that day before the discussion group officially starts, and she reverses the commute after the meeting ends. The whole process takes the entire afternoon.

2

● Working with families to overcome the negative effects of discrimination. Practitioners seek to recognize the ways in which families experience overt and subtle discrimination, to validate families' experiences, and to empower families to choose how to respond to these experiences.

Key Practice 3: Celebrate and appreciate program participants.

Although every interaction, from the welcome at the door to participation in program decision making, is a step in the relationship-building process, special events can be intentional, vital opportunities to recognize program participants. Such events are often sources of great pride to family members, and enhance families' sense of ownership of the program.

Some ways to accomplish this are:

● Using bulletin boards and newsletters to recognize family milestones and accomplishments such as a new job, the birth of a child, or the accomplishment of a life goal.

● Communicating appreciation directly through verbal and written communication. A practitioner may send a note to a family who has not been actively participating in a while, just to stay in touch and let them know that they are important to the program.

● Recognizing adults' accomplishments and contributions. Programs hold graduations or recognition ceremonies for classes or groups that meet for a specific duration. Some programs give program participants tangible symbols of appreciation such as flowers, awards, certificates, or cards. These may be presented at a special event or ceremony.

Key Practice 4: Face difficult issues with families at their own pace and on their own terms.

Families respond to stress and seek solutions in a variety of ways. Some families may use denial as a coping mechanism, while others may be driven to impulsive action. Though people under stress need help and support, they are also vulnerable, and they may be extremely sensitive to feeling pressured or intruded upon. In order to avoid alienating family members, the practitioner needs to take his or her cue on how to proceed from them, adopting a "ready-when-you-are" approach. Practitioners also recognize that response to stress typically progresses through stages, including denial and high-energy action, and strive to help families manage both the stress and their changing responses to that stress.

Some ways for programs to accomplish this are:

3

Practice Example

I didn't pay much attention to the fact that my (excellent) day care center called itself a "family care center" until after I had my second child. I had eight weeks of maternity leave, so I had temporarily withdrawn Bryan from the center. But things were really different this time. After Bryan was born, I remember crying a lot even though I knew I was happy. My midwife and my friends told me it was normal: just hormones causing "the baby blues," kind of like the letdown after a big test. It went away after a week or so. After Curtis was born, it was much worse and it didn't go away. Neither my friends nor my husband, Todd, understood.

A few days after Curtis was born, Sylvia, the family support worker at the center, called to congratulate us and to ask for a photo of Bryan and Curtis for the bulletin board. A couple of weeks later, she called to see how we were doing. I told her fine, but I also arranged to bring Bryan back the next week. I didn't say that I was worried and crying all the time, on the verge of divorce, and contemplating suicide, or that I was too anxious to take care of my kids; but she must have sensed that something was wrong. When I dropped Bryan off, Sylvia and I had coffee, privately. She was patient and gentle; I opened up. She told me about postpartum depression and gave me some handouts and the phone number of someone to talk to about a support group. I didn't do anything with that stuff right away. I was too depressed to reach out. But God love her, Sylvia kept checking in. She touched base with me every couple of days; if Todd brought Bryan in, she'd call. She was really sweet, not pressuring, just caring. After a week, I called the support group contact person and got some help.

4

GUIDELINES FOR FAMILY SUPPORT PRACTICE

● Providing direction and resources for practitioners. Programs may devote time in staff meetings to discussing difficult issues that specific families are facing and ways in which the practitioner can or should respond. Some programs provide peer-to-peer consultation time for staff. Others provide front-line workers with a trained and skilled supervisor—or professional specialist outside of the program—with whom they can consult.

● Encouraging staff members to obtain specialized training on working with families in crisis, domestic violence, substance abuse, and other mental health issues. Some programs make it possible for their staff to attend school through flexible schedules or tuition reimbursement.

● Making referrals to specialized agencies when the program's resources are insufficient to help a family member with a specific issue. In order to facilitate referrals, programs develop different kinds of relationships with other specialized agencies. These range from informal relationships between their respective staff members to formal agreements to link projects or services. Family support practitioners help families access these agencies, sometimes by accompanying them to their first appointment, or, when necessary, calling the agency directly to make an introduction.

Key Practice 5: Persevere.

Growth and development are processes that take time and are not always smooth and comfortable. Family members who are under stress, frustrated, isolated, or struggling sometimes exhibit behaviors that are difficult to work with, such as depression, extreme anger, and aggression. These difficulties are experienced by people facing a variety of circumstances, such as a new mother suffering from sleep deprivation, anxiety, and post-partum depression; an adult looking for a new job after having been laid off; and a pre-teen seeking to be accepted by peers without joining a gang. Demonstrating patience and making every effort to maintain contact reinforce the trusting relationship.

Some ways to accomplish this are:

● Maintaining contact with families. When family members miss appointments or stay away for a long time, practitioners may follow up with a phone call, a note, or a home visit. They may express concern to friends of the family, sending a message that they are cared about in their absence.

● Keeping an open, positive, problem-solving attitude. For example, practitioners strive to avoid judging families negatively when they don't follow through on stated action plans, but

Practice Example

"Dealing with situations where there is abuse is always really difficult for me. Sometimes I know the children need to be in a safer place, but when I need to report a family to child protective services, I always wonder if I've done the right thing," says Gladys, a family support worker in a low-income, urban neighborhood that is plagued by a violent drug culture. "I still think about Cassandra and her children."

Cassandra was first coaxed to the center by a home visitor who offered the center's help in securing formula, diapers, and clothing for her two young children. Cassandra had been sexually abused as a child, and was a young mother with a drug problem, a physically violent boyfriend, and a history of suicide attempts.

Cassandra trusted few people, but she seemed to like Gladys and called her and dropped in to talk about various problems. Gladys relied heavily on the advice and solace offered by "Dr. Eddie," a local psychiatrist who volunteered a few hours a week at the center. With his help, she sought treatment for Cassandra's drug and mental health problems.

After a short period of apparent improvement in Cassandra's life, she reunited with her abusive boyfriend and started getting high again. Dr. Eddie helped Gladys to understand that many of Cassandra's problems were beyond the center's ability to resolve. He and the rest of the center staff helped Gladys feel more comfortable in meeting the responsibility she knew she had to report the threat to the children's safety to social services. Cassandra's children were eventually placed in foster care.

5

E

1

rather, work with them to identify and overcome obstacles to participation and growth.

● Being dependable. Family support practitioners always make a good faith effort to follow through on what they say they will do. They take commitments to family members very seriously. If it is necessary to renegotiate appointments or commitments, they do so in advance.

> **Guideline E: Family support practitioners communicate responsibly and effectively with families.**

Practice Example

On welfare and a former substance abuser, Betty has often felt disrespected or ignored by the state social services agency workers with whom she has dealt. They have seemed to her more concerned with filling out paperwork than with helping her or her three children, who had spent a year in foster care.

Betty's friend told her about some craft classes at the family resource center at a local church that sounded fun. And best of all, the friend said, they had babysitters. Upon her arrival, Betty was enraged to be greeted by a staff person who insisted that she sign in her children at the childcare room before she could engage in the craft activities. Betty yelled and cursed at the staff person, within earshot of her (and other) children.

Anita, an experienced supervisor, gently asked Betty to come and have coffee in her office. Anita listened as Betty vented her anger. Gradually the conversation shifted from what had happened at the center door to what had happened in Betty's previous contacts with social service agencies. Anita asked lots of questions about Betty's children and spoke glowingly about some of the other children at the center that day. Everything at the center, she said, was designed with the well-being of the children in mind, including the sign-in procedures. Anita then explained some of the other protocols of the center, including the expectation that all adults would refrain from profanity while at the center for the sake of the children. Betty thanked Anita and told her that no agency worker had ever spent so much time talking to her. She also said that she had never met anyone who seemed so genuinely interested in children.

Key Practice 1: Listen empathically and pay attention to the way family members respond to what you say.

Careful listening is the primary way family support practitioners obtain the information that they need to validate a family's values, beliefs, and experiences and to guide a family toward an array of appropriate resources. Listening involves not only hearing words, but paying attention to nonverbal cues (such as body language, tone of voice, facial expression, and gestures).

Some ways to accomplish this are:

● Asking questions to clarify what has been heard. Practitioners may also repeat back what they have understood.

● Paying close attention to families' responses (both verbal and nonverbal). Practitioners learn about and seek to understand nonverbal cues in the context of a family's culture. When there seems to be confusion, practitioners use positive and encouraging language to explain things in a different way.

● Being conscious of messages conveyed by one's own nonverbal cues.

Key Practice 2: Balance supportive, accepting interaction with open, honest communication about disagreements.

A practitioner may encounter situations in which a family's or parent's actions or decisions conflict with the knowledge, values, and assumptions that the practitioner brings to the relationship. Although these situations may be difficult, they also

2

offer an opportunity to strengthen the partnership between family and practitioner. A positive result is possible when the practitioner remains supportive and accepting of the family while honestly exploring the issues on which parent and practitioner disagree.

Some ways to accomplish this are:

● Recognizing and discussing disagreements. Practitioners handle conflict honestly.

● Assisting families in exploring alternatives. Practitioners talk with families about what they want their actions to result in (for example, "good behavior" on the part of the child) and use this common understanding to discuss alternative actions and behaviors that could produce these results. This discussion includes both positive and negative potential outcomes and consequences of adopting a certain strategy or making a specific decision.

Practice Example

Brenda was raised by parents who believed in the adage "Spare the rod and spoil the child," and that's the way she was raising her four children, too. However, physical discipline was not allowed at the family resource center where Brenda attended GED classes while her children played in the childcare room.

Brenda struck up a friendship with Linda, a young staff person at the center who happened to live in the same building as Brenda and was a mother of three boys. The first time Linda observed Brenda giving one of her children a hard spanking she used it as a way to start a conversation about different ways of disciplining children and different families' attitudes about discipline. Linda took great care to ensure that Brenda saw her and the other staff people using other methods to discipline the children who came to the center. She would talk to Brenda about how children respond to constant physical discipline. At one point, Brenda suddenly told her how she felt when beaten as a child. One day Brenda said to Linda, "Before coming here I didn't know there were other ways to make my children behave."

Relationship Building: Challenges in Practice

1. Program managers and practitioners sometimes do not view a respectful, equal partnership as possible with the population of families with whom they work.

A family who upon entering a program is in the midst of a complicated crisis, or has a particular characteristic that labels them as in need of special attention, can initially present a challenge to programs and practitioners. These families at first glance may seem unlikely candidates for an equal relationship with a practitioner. The stereotypes and assumptions that such families may elicit from program staff can be substantial barriers to developing the empowering relationships that will be the most beneficial to families.

To overcome these barriers, program staff must carefully reflect on the assumptions being made about these families. What are the practitioner's reasons for resisting an equal relationship? What family strengths have been overlooked? Are there cultural, ethnic, linguistic, class, or educational factors (or biases) that contribute to staff members' judgment that families are not able to participate in an equal relationship?

It may help for program staff to understand that forming a respectful, equal relationship with a family is, in all cases, a developmental process. Even though a family may initially come to the program in crisis and in need of extensive assistance from the program, practitioners work to identify starting points for empowering the family to take charge of their own issues. It is important to recognize that everyone needs help, support, and skills to tackle new challenges. The fact that a family needs assistance should not obviate the development of an equal relationship that is based on respect.

There are families in every program who possess the skills needed to use the program's resources well and to initiate and maintain non-hierarchical, respectful relationships with staff members. One way to provide capacity-building opportunities for all participants, in this and other areas, is to encourage families with stronger skills to serve as mentors and guides. Through their relationships with these "mentor"

families, practitioners have the opportunity to model the relationships that they are trying to build with all families.

2. In practice, practitioners sometimes have difficulty being nonjudgmental and honest at the same time.

No matter how open, respectful, and accepting practitioners strive to be, there may come a time when a practitioner feels incapable of understanding, accepting, or empathizing with a particular individual's or family's experiences, lifestyles, world views, or behaviors. These differences become challenges when the practitioner's values, beliefs, and expectations come into direct conflict with those of the family.

While the family clearly has the power to make decisions about continuing with a particular practitioner, practitioners also have a choice about engaging in relationship building with a particular individual and/or family. In these cases, practitioners have a responsibility to be self-reflective in identifying why particular differences are becoming obstacles for the relationship-building process. Programs also have the responsibility to provide staff with supportive opportunities to critically examine their feelings, the actions that arise from those feelings, and alternative options for dealing with them. A program manager in such a situation has several options. He or she may decide to assign other staff to the family (either permanently or as the family deals with a particular issue), to provide support for the staff member to work through the difficulties, or to work with the family and the practitioner together on the obstacles in the relationship.

For example, a family may be struggling with a decision about abortion. A practitioner may feel that she cannot be accepting, nonjudgmental, empathic, and responsive in this situation because of her personal convictions. The response might be to say: "I appreciate how difficult this situation is for you. I have my own particular views about abortion that may make it difficult for me to help you with this decision. I would recommend that you consider talking to Harriet or Matt about it; they have been excellent resources for other families facing in your situation."

Conflicts also arise when the program as a whole is

unwilling to tolerate certain behaviors or beliefs. Many programs find that a policy or rule about behaviors that are acceptable within the program are best developed after careful examination, dialogue, and input from all stakeholders, including staff and family participants. If a particular behavior is deemed unacceptable, all involved must consider how to respond to the behavior when it arises and what options may be presented to the family or individual in order to ensure that they have choices about their participation. For example, a program that decides, after considerable discussion with everyone involved, that the use of foul language is inappropriate in program interactions might suggest that a staff member approach families in violation of the policy in this way: "After a great deal of consideration, parents and staff in our program decided that use of curse words is not acceptable within the program. We feel that we need to create a setting that is respectful of others as a way of modeling respect for our children. I would very much like to work with you as a resource in helping you meet your goals. Could you live with this rule while you're in the program?"

3. Even though everyone acknowledges that building relationships takes time and effort, practitioners are sometimes expected to work with too many families and have little time to develop the types of relationships necessary for effective assistance.

Program managers bear responsibility for arranging working conditions, job responsibilities, and schedules that allow staff members to work at the optimum level with families. Their expectations for top-quality job performance need to take into consideration the amount of time necessary for relationships to develop and the limitations that the program's policies may place on the staff's ability to perform effectively. With too many families and not enough time, effective relationships will take longer to develop.

As part of the effort to create an effective program, managers must strive to be realistic about their expectations of themselves and their staff members; they also must identify the sources of pressures to over-estimate their capacity and to over-extend their staff. Program managers have the option of

working to educate the program's funders about the necessity of adequate time for staff and families to develop effective relationships. Programs may need to reject contracts or grants that set unrealistic service goals. This kind of advocacy is essential to ensure quality practice.

4. Sometimes very serious situations occur that require action on the part of the practitioner or program which might jeopardize the relationship with a given family.

In the course of family support practice, a range of conflicts between families and programs are possible. Sometimes a family continually violates the rules of the program and causes difficulties and discomfort to other program participants. Sometimes family members repeatedly do things that jeopardize their progress towards their goals. Sometimes a family support worker sees or hears something that makes him or her think that a family member is in serious physical or emotional danger.

A situation which places one or more people or the entire program in jeopardy requires that the practitioner confront the family immediately and directly to discuss the consequences of their actions. It is always the practitioner's desire to act with honesty, empathy, and compassion and to try to strengthen the relationship that she or he has built with the family and that the family has built with the program. The ideal course of action is to discuss the situation with the family, making sure to explain the rules and the consequences of ignoring those rules clearly; and to assist families in exploring alternatives. To be responsible and effective in this type of situation, however, practitioners must be extremely skilled in confrontation, and they must recognize that it is sometimes not possible to maintain a good relationship with a family, eliminate a threat of danger, and comply with government and program mandates all at once.

It is the program's responsibility to provide appropriate training and effective supervision for staff members and to make sure that staff members who do not have expertise in this area have access to someone who does. Programs should assure staff members that when they are unsure of how to proceed it is always appropriate to consult a supervisor or other person who has appropriate professional expertise. Program managers are responsible for ensuring compliance with the state's laws and mandates.

5. Family members do not always speak with one voice. Building relationships with families may be especially complicated by conflicts between family members.

As any member of a family understands, family members may share goals and values but disagree with one another on specific issues. Family members frequently have needs that conflict with the needs of other family members. For example, it is common for the personal needs of parents and children to conflict: a mother may need time for herself or to obtain a job that produces more income for the family, her child may need her to spend more time with him. In some families, there are long-standing issues and animosities between certain family members. These facts of life complicate practitioners' efforts to build relationships with families.

Programs that seek to involve primarily unmarried teen parents as program participants illustrate most dramatically the kinds of family conflicts that sometimes present great challenges for practitioners. For an unmarried teen mom, the family constellation often includes not only herself and her child but her parents, grandparents, and other relatives, as well as the father of the child and the father's parents. Each of these family members has a distinct point of view about what the young mother should do with her life and with the child, and the potential for conflict among the points of view is high. The young mother's participation in the program may be a point of conflict among competing family members; her relationship with the practitioner may be viewed as a threat to the authority or ability of other family members to help her. The father of the child may feel shut out of a significant relationship with his child if there is no support for his participation. The practitioner may be viewed as "taking sides" with one faction in the family, even if the practitioner is unaware of the conflict. The practitioner cannot effectively work to empower the young mother to deal with competing demands in her life without understanding all of the different points of view represented and how they affect the mother and her child.

When practitioners work directly with all family members, conflicts between family members may make it difficult for the practitioner to establish an effective relationship. Family members may have conflicting—and unspoken—views about aspects of child rearing, about what the family's goals should be, or about who makes decisions within the family. The estranged parents of a child may both participate in the program, and both may be concerned about sustaining a loving relationships with their child, although not with each other.

As a result of any of these situations, one member of the family may feel supported and validated by the practitioner's assistance while another may feel threatened and undermined. The practitioner's challenge is to continue to reach out to each member of the family, understanding that relationship building happens on an individual basis as well as a family one.

Over time, the practitioner's persistence in seeking to understand the family's wishes, working in partnership with the family on issues that all family members agree are important, supporting the family as these issues surface, and assisting the family in dealing with their conflicts can be rewarded with an effective relationship with each person and with the whole family. The practitioner's vigilance in understanding the potential for conflict and in consistently respecting differing points of view within the family can be a positive factor in establishing a long-term, trusting relationship with all of the family members. Conflict offers opportunities for modeling respectful listening, identifying and examining points of disagreement, and working to resolve these points of disagreement in ways that support each family member.

When a family member's physical or emotional safety is threatened by another family member, the practitioner may be required to "side" with the member who needs protection. In this case, the practitioner acts to ensure the immediate safety of each family member by whatever means are necessary, including asking for assistance from law enforcement or child protection workers.

Principle Two
Programs enhance families' capacity to support the growth and development of all family members—adults, youth, and children.

Principle Three
Families are resources to their own members, to other families, to programs, and to communities.

The ultimate goal of family-supportive practice is to promote the healthy development of children. The healthy development of children is dependent on the healthy development of their families. When programs promote optimal development, they assume that there is already a process of growth and development under way in families, and that families have skills, knowledge, and resources to "bank on." The role of family support programs is to help families identify, enhance, and utilize their existing skills, knowledge, and resources in the ongoing task of promoting a healthy environment for their family members.

Enhancing Families' Ability to Nurture

While every family is different, each family bears responsibility for providing what its members need to develop in a healthy way. Tangible necessities such as shelter, food, physical safety, economic security, health care, and education are important for every family member's development. Consistent nurturing, care giving, cognitive stimulation, emotional safety, a sense of the family's history and values, and opportunities for quality social interaction are equally important. Family members, from infants to the elderly, need additional, specific kinds of support as they work through different stages of development and encounter a variety of experiences.

Typically, families are able to provide many of the concrete necessities that provide a basis for healthy development, but they often encounter more barriers to providing an environment for children in which they are consistently nurtured. Parents today are often stressed by rapidly changing family structures, conflicting expectations of them, economic pressures, and increased isolation from extended families. Low-income families often encounter systemic barriers to obtaining resources; discrimination based on racial, cultural, and socio-economic differences; and limited ability to influence legal and political systems. These stresses may further reduce the energy and time that parents have to contribute to their children's development.

Effective parenting requires time, energy, knowledge, and skills, which are available in varying degrees depending upon family members' circumstances and ages. Every family has experienced a time when meeting all family members' needs seemed overwhelming and impossible. Occasions that bring change within the family, such as the birth of a child, a divorce, or the death of a grandparent, can create new demands while diminishing the time, energy, and money that the family has to meet those demands.

Family support programs offer families a number of strategies for enhancing their capacity to support their own healthy development. Many are designed for those times when the need for additional support is high. Programs often offer services and assistance that serve as families' pathways to obtaining concrete resources, such as job training, food stamps, and special services for children with disabilities. Family support programs work with families in crisis to meet their immediate needs for housing and medical care; they also help families improve the home environment in which their members are nurtured.

The Importance of Parents in Children's Development

Families' capacity to support their own development is important because optimal child development depends on the family's ability to contribute effectively to the developmental process. The significance of the parent in child development has been well documented, especially in the past three decades. From the time a child is born, a strong parent-child relationship is a major factor in his or her development. Early infant stimulation and high-quality interaction between the infant and the parent or caregiver have been linked with many positive outcomes for children.[1] Parents are widely recognized as children's first and most important teachers, who foster children's readiness for formal learning experiences and school achievement.

Several studies have recognized that access to a range of resources and sources of support enhances parents' self-confidence and their capacity to nurture their children.[2] This appears to lead to academic achievement and other indicators of positive development for children—even for those children born after their parents' contact with the programs that provided the services and supports had ceased.[3] Head Start programs have provided additional evidence that parents are vital resources for their children's development.[4] Education reform studies show that, in addition to parents' contributions during early childhood, parents' involvement in their children's schooling leads to children's success in school.[5] The overwhelming importance of parents to children's development implies that effective programs that are concerned with child development must reach out to support parents.

Building on Strengths to Enhance Capacity

A number of studies have examined effective ways to assist families in their development. A strengths-based approach that treats families as their own best resources seems to be the most effective approach, because it enhances confidence, improves parents' capacity for coping with the stresses of daily life as well as crises, and improves families' ability to access the resources they possess as well as external ones. These are all important elements in the family's capacity to support the ongoing development of its members.[6] A strengths-based approach provides opportunities for families to assess the skills and knowledge they already have, experience success in using them in small ways, and then move for-

ward to solve bigger problems. For families who have experienced many barriers to success and few opportunities to identify their strengths and use them effectively, this approach is critical.[7]

African American scholars and practitioners have had a vital influence on the adoption of a strengths-based approach in family support practice. They first raised concerns in the 1960s about negative myths, stereotypes, and self-fulfilling prophecies and their harmful effects on the development of African American children and families. They argued that strengths, rather than deficits, provide a more appropriate lens for understanding and working effectively with families who are not of the dominant culture.[8] This position has been embraced by family support programs and adopted as an essential way of working with all families. For example, all families have skills, knowledge, and commitments that are recognized as assets within their own culture, but these are not necessarily recognized as strengths in the dominant culture or in traditional methods of assessing families' capacity. Programs that strive to enhance families' capacity to foster their children's development cannot be successful without looking for, understanding, and building on these inherent strengths. Ways of identifying and building on strengths that are culturally defined continue to be discovered and refined in the context of family support practice.[9]

Families Are Resources to Themselves and Others

A person's single most important resource is usually her or his family; the family typically provides both concrete and emotional support that others cannot provide. In particular, parents are powerful people in children's lives (e.g., they provide their children's material necessities, serve as their children's teachers, and mediate their children's experiences in the outside world). Families impart to children their culture, history, beliefs, values, and a sense of belonging, and point the child toward the identity that he or she develops.

One source of strength that virtually every family has is an informal network of friends, relatives, neighbors, and co-workers to whom they turn for resources and support.[10]

Building on this strength is particularly important because mutually satisfying, reciprocal relationships such as those that constitute these informal networks are vital resources for personal development. Membership in a network of support enhances family members' sense of self-worth by encouraging them to perceive themselves as worthy of the concern of others.[11] Self-help and mutual aid groups have had positive, long-lasting effects on those members' families and communities.[12] The positive effects of these supportive relationships on parents and children have been well documented.[13]

Families are resources to their own members and to others. They participate in networks of extended family, neighbors, friends, and coworkers who reciprocally provide day-to-day assistance and support in times of trouble. Family support programs help families to build their supportive networks. They encourage participants to serve as mentors and advocates for other families, volunteers for program activities, and board members. They also promote families' roles as resources in the community outside of the program by encouraging them to be leaders on community-wide issues, from neighborhood clean-up to legislative issues that affect families in the community.

NOTES

[1] Shonkoff, J. (1987) "Family beginnings: Infancy and support." In S. L. Kagan, D. R. Powell, B. Weissbourd, and E. F. Zigler, eds., *America's family support programs: Perspectives and prospects.* (New Haven, Conn.: Yale University Press) 79–98.

[2] Heinecke, C. M. (1991) In D. Unger and D. R. Powell, eds., *Families as nurturing systems: Support across the life span.* (New York: Hawthorne Press) 127–142.

[3] Seitz, V. and N. H. Apfel (1994) "Parent-focused intervention: Diffusion effects on siblings." *Child Development* 65 (2) 677–683.

[4] Zigler, E. and W. Berman (1983) "Discerning the future of early childhood intervention." *American Psychologist* 38 (8) 894–906.

[5] Epstein, J. (1987) "Toward a theory of family-school connection: Teacher practices and parent involvement." In K. Hurrelmann, F. Kaufman, and F. Losel, *Social interaction: Potential and constraints.* (Berlin: Walter de Gruyter Press).

[6] Zigler, E. and K. B. Black (1989) "America's family support movement: Strengths and limitations." *American Journal of Orthopsychiatry* 59 (1) 6–19.

Dunst, C. J., C. M. Trivette, and A. G. Deal (1994) "Resource-based family-centered intervention practices." In C. J. Dunst, C. M. Trivette, and A. G. Deal, eds., *Supporting and strengthening families, Vol. 1: Methods, strategies, and practices.* (Cambridge, Mass.: Brookline Books) 141–151.

Stoneman, Z. (1985) "Family involvement in early childhood special education programs." In N. H. Fallen and W. Umansky, eds., *Young children with special needs.* (2nd edition) (Columbus, Ohio: Charles E. Merril) 442–469.

[7] Rappaport, J. (1981) "In praise of paradox: A social policy of empowerment over prevention." *American Journal of Community Psychology* 9 (1) 1–25.

Hobbs, N., P. R. Dokecki, K. V. Hoover-Dempey, R. M. Moroney, M. W. Shayne, and K. H. Weeks (1984) *Strengthening families.* (San Francisco, Calif.: Jossey-Bass).

Dunst, C. J., C. M. Mott, and D. W. Mott (1994) "Strengths-based intervention practices." In C. J. Dunst, C. M. Trivette, and A. G. Deal, eds., *Supporting and strengthening families, Vol. 1: Methods, strategies, and practices.* (Cambridge, Mass.: Brookline Books) 115–131.

[8] Billingsley, A. (1968) *Black families in white America.* (Englewood Cliffs, N.J.: Prentice Hall).

ENHANCING FAMILY CAPACITY

Hill, R. (1972) *The strengths of Black families.* (New York: Emerson Hall Publishers).

[9] Kagan, S. L. and A. Shelley (1987) "The promise and problems of family support programs." In S. L. Kagan, D. R. Powell, B. Weissbourd, and E. Zigler, eds., *America's family support programs: Perspectives and prospects.* (New Haven, Conn.: Yale University Press) 3–18.

Powell, D. R. (1995) "Including Latino fathers in parent education and support programs: Development of a program model." In R. E. Zambrana, ed., *Understanding Latino families: Scholarship, policy, and practice.* (Thousand Oaks, Calif.: Sage Publications, Inc.) 85–106.

Nobles, W. W. (1988) "African-American family life: An instrument of culture." In H. McAdoo, ed., *Black families,* (*second edition*). (Thousand Oaks, Calif.: Sage Publications, Inc.) 44–53.

[10] Gottlieb, B. H. (1981) *Social networks and social support.* (*4th edition*). (Thousand Oaks, Calif.: Sage Publications).

Whittaker, J. K., J. Garbarino, and Associates (1983) *Social support networks: Informal helping in the human services.* (New York: Aldine Publishing Co.).

[11] Ibid., 64.

[12] Powell, D. R. and J. Elsenstadt (1988) "Informal and formal conversation in parent discussion groups: An observational study." *Family Relations* (37) 166–170.

[13] Cochran, M., M. Larner, D. Riley, L. Gunnarrson, and C. Henderson (1990) *Extending families: The social networks of parents and their children.* (New York: Cambridge University Press).

Hobbs, N., P. R. Dokecki, K. V. Hoover-Dempey, R. M. Moroney, M. W. Shayne, and K. H. Weeks (1984) *Strengthening families.* (San Francisco, Calif.: Jossey-Bass).

Crnic, K. A., M. T. Greenberg, A. Ragozin, N. Robinson, and R. Bashman (1983) "Effects of stress and social support on mothers of premature and full-term infants." *Child Development* 54 (1) 209–217.

Crockenberg, S. B. (1981) "Infant irritability, mother responsiveness and social influences on the security of infant-mother attachment." *Child Development* 52 (3) 857–865.

Dunst, C. J. and C. M. Trivette (1986) "Looking beyond the parent-child dyad for the determinants of maternal styles of interaction." *Infant Mental Health Journal* 7 (1) 69–80.

Dunst, C. J., C. M. Trivette, and A. H. Cross (1986) "Mediating influences of social support: Personal, family, and child outcomes." *American Journal of Mental Deficiency* 90, (4) 403–424.

Trivette, C. M. and C. J. Dunst (1987) "Proactive influences of social support in families of handicapped children." In H. G. Lingren, L. Kimmons, P. Lee, G. Rowe, L. Rottman, L. Schwab, and R. Williams, eds., *Family Strengths, Vol. 8-9, Pathways to well-being.* (Lincoln, Nebr.: University of Nebraska Press) 391–405.

Dunst, C. J. and C. M. Trivette (1988) "A family systems model of early intervention with handicapped and developmentally at-risk children." In D. R. Powell, ed., *Parent education as early childhood intervention: Emerging directions in theory, research, and practice.* (Norwood, N.J.: Ablex Publishing Co.) 131–180.

Vega, W. A. and B. Kolody (1985) "The meaning of social support and the mediation of stress across cultures." In W. A. Vega and M. Miranda, eds., *Stress and Hispanic mental health* (DHHS Publication No. 85-1410). (Rockville, Md.: National Institute of Mental Health) 48–75.

Enhancing Family Capacity: Guidelines for Practice

Some family support programs serve families who have considerable control over their lives; the parents come to the program to talk about their child-raising concerns with other parents or to develop friendships for themselves and their children. They experience the usual life stresses and seek an opportunity to be with others dealing with similar issues. Other programs serve families who are under inordinate stress; these parents look to the program for assistance in meeting their basic needs and in learning ways to improve the quality of life for themselves and their children. All family support programs, regardless of the families they serve, build on the strengths of family members and the positive aspects of their family life. Specific planning responds to each family's needs, and the intensity of staff involvement varies in accordance with the nature and degree of stress family members are experiencing.

Guidelines and Key Practices

Guideline A: **Family support practitioners develop with family members a full understanding of a family's strengths.**

Key Practices
1. Work with family members to identify their existing competencies and past successes.
2. Encourage all family members to participate in the program.
3. Help families identify and acknowledge informal networks of support and culturally specific resources.

Guideline B: **Programs create opportunities for parents—both fathers and mothers—to enhance the parent-child relationship.**

Key Practices
1. Provide a variety of resources to inform parents about child development, the parent-child relationship, and parenting issues.
2. Maximize opportunities for parents—both mothers and fathers—and children to work and play together.

Guideline C: **When family members express a desire to resolve problems or to change something about their lives, practitioners work with them to develop a realistic plan of action that is tailored to their strengths, needs, priorities, and resources and support them during the process of implementing that plan.**

Key Practices
1. Help family members identify sources of stress in their lives and ways to relieve or reduce that stress.
2. Work with families to set realistic goals when they seek to make changes in their life situation.
3. Create opportunities for families to gain information and learn new life skills.
4. Reinforce strengths while families are dealing with challenges or working towards goals.
5. Facilitate families' decision to "move on" when the program has met their needs or when they need something the program does not offer.

Guideline D: **Programs approach parents as significant resources for each other and for the program.**

Key Practices
1. Ensure that parent input shapes all aspects of the program.
2. Facilitate mutually helpful peer-to-peer relationships among program participants.

A

1

Guideline A: Family support practitioners develop with family members a full understanding of a family's strengths.

Key Practice 1: Work with family members to identify their existing competencies and past successes.

Family support practitioners believe that all family members have things that they do well, triumphs in their pasts, and the potential to expand on their strengths and successes to achieve their goals. Identifying strengths is a prerequisite to building on strengths. Involving families in articulating their strengths helps improve parents' self-esteem, boosts their belief in their own competence, and gives even demoralized families hope for the future. In family support practice, practitioners and families identify strengths together through ongoing conversations and contact.

Some ways to accomplish this are:

- Looking for strengths in every interaction with family members. Parents tell stories about their lives; recount past experiences; and talk about their dreams, disappointments, values, and preferences. Family support practitioners help family members glean insight into their strengths from these stories.

- Asking families open-ended questions. Practitioners ask parents about their past experiences with achieving goals and solving problems, daily routines, and ways of interacting with and responding to each other and others.

- Observing family functioning and interaction. Formal program components such as family literacy classes and parent-child interaction opportunities, and informal activities such as parties and potlucks, enable practitioners to observe family strengths to build on. For example, they might notice that a mother is exceptionally tuned-in to her child's behavior and that she responds sensitively to the child, that a father has a strong sense of ethnic identity and is communicating both traditions and pride to his child, or that mom and dad seem to be sending consistent messages. Sometimes visiting families at their homes allows practitioners to see strengths that might not be visible otherwise. For example, parents might have a collection of books and a desk and chair for their school-aged children, which would signify that they want their children to

Practice Example

My husband and I put off starting a family until our careers were firmly established. I had been a successful advertising executive with many satisfied clients. Believing myself to be smart and effective with clients who often acted like children, I was sure I'd be a wonderful parent.

All that changed when my son was born. It seemed like he wanted to nurse twenty-four hours a day. I rarely had two hours of continuous sleep. In my previous life, I would have accomplished ten different things before eleven a.m. Now I felt lucky if I could take a shower and throw on a different pair of sweats. I felt fat and ugly. And the only feedback I received from my son was negative. He cried for hours, especially if I tried to put him down. No client, no boss had ever made me feel so stupid, ineffective, and helpless. Like my son, I spent a lot of time in tears.

At my six-week post-partum checkup, the nurse-midwife recognized my despair and encouraged me to visit a local family resource center. I spent most of my first visit with Melissa spilling my guts in between sobs. It felt good to have a shoulder to cry on. Melissa reassured me that my baby's behavior was perfectly normal and that my reactions were also. She suggested that I talk to other parents and told me about a support group for new parents at the center. We talked about concrete things that I could do to take care of myself, especially when I was feeling overwhelmed.

The next time, I went to the center during drop-in hours, with my son, Charlie. Things had started to shape up, thanks to Melissa's suggestions. As we talked, Melissa asked to hold Charlie. When she took him, he started to cry. To quiet him, I suggested she hold him upright instead of cradling him. "You know, it seems to me that you know much more about what makes this baby tick than you give yourself credit for," she said. "And maybe the reason he doesn't want you to put him down is because that's his way of telling you that he wants to be with you." I had never thought about it that way before. I couldn't help but smile. It was my first positive job review in weeks!

succeed in school, and that they know something about what their children need in order to do so and are able to provide these things.

- Videotaping family interaction and using these videos as opportunities for families to build their capacity to recognize and validate their own strengths. Practitioners recognize that it is difficult for many people to watch themselves on videotape and are careful to create a constructive, safe, and non-judgmental climate for the discussion.

Key Practice 2: Encourage all family members to participate in the program.

Family support practitioners recognize that in many families, parents and children are only part of the story. Grandparents, aunts and uncles, godparents, and any friend who plays a role in the family can strongly influence the children's growth and can provide additional strengths and resources to the family. Family support programs invite and welcome the participation of all people identified by a family as part of the family.

Some ways to accomplish this are:

- Asking participants to define their families. Practitioners explicitly ask families to list all of the people whom they consider family, including all of those who are most significant in their lives.

- Targeting some activities to specific family members such as fathers, siblings, grandparents, or godparents.

- Encouraging participants to help in outreach activities and planning of events and activities that appeal to different groups. For example, grandparents are wonderful resources and can provide help for programs in diverse ways ranging from storytelling to children, to "looking in" on families, to organizing quilting or knitting projects or teaching others the craft. A musician on the block may tutor youth; a carpenter may build attractive and functional childcare storage bins. One young adult may solicit others for clean-up work.

_2_

Practice Example

At our staff meetings, we regularly discuss what's going right with the center and what things could work better. A while ago, many of us were troubled by the fact that fathers weren't participating in our activities to any great extent. We decided to ask some moms and dads why the men weren't coming to the center. Some dads complained that the center looked like a "woman's place." All the posters, artwork, and messages on the wall were about women. And there were no male staff. This reinforced the commonly held idea that parenting was "woman's work." Together, staff and parents came up with some recommendations to change this, and we have been able to implement almost all of them.

First, we hired some men. The new male staff went out to where the men hung out. They got to know some of the dads, uncles, and grandfathers of the neighborhood children at the car repair shop, at the basketball courts, and at the factory—the community's biggest employer. A few of those men got involved. They scheduled some basketball games under the center's sponsorship. They also got permission to use some of the center's space to build a workout room, which many of the men wanted. More men started coming to the center. Soon, pictures of dads in various activities appeared all over the center. A group of dads have started a support group of their own at the center. And now many more of our all-family activities have both moms and dads participating.

Key Practice 3: Help families identify and acknowledge informal networks of support and culturally specific resources.

Informal support is vital to any family's ability to function well. Generally, when families feel connected to other people and/or to religious or cultural traditions they feel more supported and stronger than when they are alienated and alone. In addition to helping families identify their strengths, practitioners also help families view informal relationships as resources, and as examples of their ability to take initiative and make connections. Feelings of isolation can be reduced when

_3_

ENHANCING FAMILY CAPACITY

individuals recognize the potential resources of relationships with friends, neighbors, other parents at the children's school or childcare center, fellow members of a church or social or recreational club, or coworkers. (For more information on helping families identify and access informal support in their communities, see chapter 5, guideline B.)

Some ways to accomplish this are:

Practice Example

The saying "you can't judge a book by its cover" certainly holds true for many of the young women I have worked with over the years. I am a home visitor for a family support program in an impoverished, inner-city neighborhood.

Take Anna, for example. On the surface, the situation was bleak. Anna was a twenty-year-old mother of three young children. She had never finished high school. She was on welfare and had very few employable skills. When I met her, she had a boyfriend, the father of her youngest child, who was also unemployed. He seemed to have several other girlfriends and was not a regular part of the family. Severely depressed and experiencing health problems brought on by obesity, Anna rarely left the apartment, and neither did her children.

Despite these obstacles, Anna had a few things going for her, too. She had a very supportive, caring sister who was actually the one to initiate contact between our program and Anna. Anna's sister loved her and the children and was willing to take action on their behalf.

Other assets were readily apparent after my first visit. Anna seemed to welcome my company and gradually began to talk to me about her life. I thought that—with support and encouragement—she would be receptive to getting out of the house, coming to the center, and meeting other people. Her obvious love and concern for her children was her greatest strength. She watched them like a hawk, and nothing escaped her attention. She conveyed her fears that something was wrong with her youngest son: he didn't do things as well or as quickly as her other two children did at the same age. It turns out that he was developmentally delayed.

I was able to encourage Anna to come to the center so that we could help her work on her son's development. With the support of her sister and me, Anna is now a regular at our program and has started making friends here. She is working on her reading and math skills and lately has expressed interest in starting a diet and exercise program. Anna's son enjoys coming to the center. He plays happily with other children and is receiving individualized help from a specialist in developmental delays.

- Talking with families about their cultural, religious, and familial traditions and about what allegiances and affiliations make them feel supported and connected.

- Asking parents about arrangements that they've made with friends and neighbors, such as carpooling or having someone watch the house or keep an eye out for neighborhood safety. Often families don't view these people as resources, and don't view their ability to make these arrangements as a sign of their own resourcefulness and strength. Practitioners help families recognize the support that these people have given in the past.

- Brainstorming with families. Practitioners sometimes ask parents to generate lists of people whom they know and how they know them or ways they could improve communication with them. They may discuss how to overcome barriers to accessing informal resources. They encourage families to include in these lists people such as neighbors, spiritual leaders, and natural community helpers.

- Using tools to map informal resources. Practitioners find tools such as questionnaires about natural supports, ecomaps, and genograms[1] extremely helpful in identifying family connections to sources of support. Some programs adapt these tools to identify culturally specific strengths and resources. For example, practitioners working with Latino families understand that many Latino families have large extended families that include non-blood or marriage-related "kin" and that it is common for immigrant Latino families to have complex, binational, extra-household linkages and patterns of helpful exchange. A tool that asks parents to identify family members might be adapted to appropriately include people in these networks.

---

[1] Both can be created with families to gather information and work with them to analyze their situations. A genogram is a family tree that records information about family members and their relationships over at least three generations. [McGoldrick, M. (1985) *Genograms in family assessment.* (New York: W. W. Norton).] An ecomap maps in a dynamic way the ecological system whose boundaries encompass the person or family; it pictures the family in its life situation. [Hartman, A. (1983) *Family-centered social work and practice.* (New York: The Free Press).]

GUIDELINES FOR FAMILY SUPPORT PRACTICE

Guideline B: Programs create opportunities for parents—both fathers and mothers—to enhance the parent-child relationship.

B
1

Key Practice 1: Provide a variety of resources to inform parents about child development, the parent-child relationship, and parenting issues.

One of the primary reasons some parents participate in home-visiting or center-based family support programs is to learn about child development and child rearing. Parents seek information about the stages in a child's development so that they may better understand the meaning of their children's behavior, have realistic expectations, and respond appropriately. Parents say that acquiring knowledge increases their competence and sense of confidence in their child-rearing roles. For information to be effective and valuable, it must be accessible and relevant, so programs provide a range of educational materials and resources to meet the needs of the families served.

Some ways to accomplish this are:

● Offering formal parent education opportunities tailored to parents' expressed interests and desires. Many programs offer workshops or classes on child development and infancy, toddlerhood, and preschool years, and on particular areas of interest including sleeping, toileting, discipline, and nutritional needs. For school-age years, programs may offer classes on homework assistance or children's friendships. Programs may offer classes on toy and book making and alternative ideas for children's play. Some programs provide home visits that focus on parent education.

● Providing informal opportunities for parents to learn from staff and other parents. Some programs are drop-in programs or schedule drop-in hours in which parents can talk to staff and other parents about whatever issues or concerns are on their minds. Program participants form parent support groups or rap groups to discuss topics of concern to them. Families share information with each other by developing materials such as parent education curricula and children's books.

● Modeling a healthy parent-child relationship. Program staff model positive ways of reacting to children, including methods of praising and disciplining, strategies for handling children's anger or frustration and helping them to do the same, and ways to respond with age-appropriate expectations.

● Talking with parents about being parents. Many parents seek information from practitioners on

Practice Example

At forty, I'm an older mother. My daughter, Shayna, is two, but most of my friends' children are in high school. They don't even remember their children's early years, and I feel like the stupid rookie mom asking them questions. I spent a lot of time scratching through the library for information on child development.

When Shayna was about eight months old, I saw a sign at the library announcing a five-week parent/child workshop. Shayna and I went and it was great. Dalia, one of the librarians, led the workshop. She pointed out all the things I was doing right and made me feel like there is no stupid question. Every question I asked helped me understand more about my child and made me a better mom. I learned to think about Shayna's crying as the only way she had to tell me what she needed; she wasn't being bad. Dalia helped me find resources on child development and appropriate books to read to Shayna (all kids' books are not the same!). Perhaps the nicest thing was that I met a couple of other older mothers who live close by. After the workshop ended, we signed up together for the "Mother Goose" program (to brush up on our nursery rhymes). Then we started an informal play group.

Now I'm going to a workshop for parents of toddlers. What a big difference it makes once you understand that for a two-year-old saying "no" all the time is about becoming independent and asserting herself: Shayna's not trying to be the boss or to control me. The bottom line is that these workshops have helped me respond to my child more patiently and lovingly than I might have otherwise. But Shayna ... she comes for the stories!

ENHANCING FAMILY CAPACITY

their child-rearing patterns. Practitioners can help them recognize how certain of their behaviors support their children's development. When families identify problem situations, practitioners talk with them about why they do what they do and explore with them alternative strategies for reaching the goals they desire for their children's behavior. Practitioners help parents recognize how their children respond to their actions and reactions. For example, the practitioner might discuss with a mother of a four-year-old how her responses to her son's drawing affect the child: How would he react if the mother praised specific aspects of the drawing and talked with him about them? If the mother replied with a disinterested "that's nice"? If she seemed displeased with it and asked him to draw it again?

● Assembling an on-site library. Programs compile a variety of written materials in different languages and at different literacy levels that correspond to the needs of the families whom they serve. Many programs also have audio-visual materials.

● Collaborating and exchanging resources with other programs.

Key Practice 2: Maximize opportunities for parents—both mothers and fathers—and children to work and play together.

Parent-child relationships are enhanced when families have positive experiences working or playing together. Programs recognize that parents' time, energy, and resources are limited and often prevent or curtail these types of activities; thus programs create opportunities and provide facilities and resources to promote parent-child interaction. When activities are designed for parents and children together, parents can enjoy being with their children, and they learn from observing and talking with other families and staff members.

Some ways to accomplish this are:

● Providing program activities in which parents and children interact. Many programs form parent-child play groups and/or workshops in which parents and children together develop toys, books, crafts, and other materials for their own use or for use by program participants. Programs also host social events such as family picnics, field trips, special dinners, and holiday celebrations, and plan volunteer activities for the entire family, such as painting or decorating the resource center, planting a community garden, cleaning up a local park, or creating and performing a pageant or play (perhaps for the elderly at a nearby nursing home). Programs that provide home visits often incorporate parent-child interaction as part of the visits.

● Offering space and a variety of materials that parents and

2

Practice Example

Maia and Daniel are the parents of two school-age girls. Recently, because of layoffs at their companies, they've both had to work longer and longer hours, significantly reducing the time they have with the family. A few months ago, Maia's boss told her team about a series of brown bag workshops on balancing work and family life. The workshops were co-sponsored by her company and the Grant Park Family Center. Since they were held at her workplace, during lunchtime, she decided to go.

"The workshops have helped me get the most out of the free time we have," says Maia. "Dan and I get home from work after the girls have eaten dinner. All we want to do is watch TV, so now we all watch at least a half-hour together and talk about it, especially what the programs and ads are saying about African Americans and other people of color, how girls and women are being portrayed, and what we think about it all. Then, while Dan and I are eating dinner, we help the girls with their homework."

Maia also learned about a Thursday night program at their local YMCA, designed by the parents of the Grant Park Family Center. "There's a buffet, catered by a local Black-owned restaurant. Dinner is out all evening because families arrive at different times. It's great. No cooking, no cleaning up," says Maia. "and we eat as a family." After dinner, parents and kids participate together in everything from volleyball and basketball to book discussion groups, homework help sessions, and photography classes.

"It's not the total solution. I still wish we could work less," says Maia. "But I do feel like we have a better balance now."

children can use together. These may be used in formal program activities such as parent-child play groups or during informal drop-in times. Many programs also arrange for lending or swapping of toys and children's books that parents and children can use at home.

● Exploring with parents natural opportunities for play and interaction. Practitioners suggest that parents and children set aside time to work and play together by sharing daily routines such as shopping, cooking, cleaning, and homework. Families may also be encouraged to institute regular "rituals" such as family reading times, dinner together, or special Saturday breakfasts. Practitioners may discuss with parents ways in which they can use household items for educational and play purposes, for example, using pots and pans and food items for counting and classification. Practitioners also brainstorm with parents about ways to overcome barriers to interacting with their children.

> **Guideline C: When family members express a desire to take action to resolve problems or to change something about their lives, practitioners work with them to develop a realistic plan that is tailored to their strengths, needs, priorities, and resources and support them during the process of implementing that plan.**

Practice Example

My husband, Jeff, and I moved here six years ago. Even though it meant leaving my college friends, I was happy. The weather's fine. We could afford a house. And my baby sister, Kelly, lived here—she was becoming a physical therapist. Jeff and I both wanted a big family; I've had four kids in five years!

Last year was really rough. Jeff was working himself ragged, trying to make partner at the law firm. I had three kids in diapers. But we were basically okay. We had each other. We had terrific children.

Then my baby sister died. Suddenly, in a car accident. And I just went to pieces. I felt so alone. One day I was outside in the yard with all the kids and I just sat down on the stoop and started sobbing. I remember Anna, my oldest, coming over and saying, "Mommy, what's wrong? I'm sorry. I'm sorry." I knew I needed some help. I don't remember how I learned about the family resource center. A flyer in the supermarket? A neighbor? Anyway, they were really there for me. I relied on their respite childcare. I got some counseling. They helped me talk to the kids about what was going on. They had a volunteer system where if you have a baby or a family crisis, other families will bring you dinners. With their support, I was able to get on top of my life again. Now I'm part of the community. I go for the mom-and-tot play group and to see friends. And, because I'm so grateful for all that baked ziti and lasagna they brought me, I also help out with the meals program!

Key Practice 1: Help family members identify sources of stress in their lives and ways to relieve or reduce that stress.

Stressors in parents' lives can diminish the time and energy they have available for nurturing each other and their children. When families find effective ways to reduce their level of tension and cope with inescapable pressures, relationships between family members and overall family functioning are enhanced. The practitioner's role is to "be there" for the family, to be a supportive ally, particularly during stressful times. Family members count on the support of the practitioner in order to progress in the directions in which they seek to go.

Some ways to accomplish this are:

● Listening empathically. By listening attentively and offering parents the opportunity to reflect on their situations and to analyze and explore the difficulties in their lives, practitioners assist parents in discovering strategies for negotiating and alleviating stress.

● Providing emotional support. Practitioners are available to parents, are interested in their concerns, and express confidence in their potential to solve problems. Practitioners assure family members that their communication will be two-way and that they do not have to wait for the

E N H A N C I N G   F A M I L Y   C A P A C I T Y

practitioner to get in touch with them. Practitioners check in with families regularly and may call with words of encouragement, or drop by families' homes or other places where they are likely to be.

● Supporting family members in the processes of brainstorming alternative strategies for dealing with challenging situations and creating realistic plans of action to resolve problems.

2

Key Practice 2: Work with families to set realistic goals when they seek to make changes in their life situations.

Practice Example

Around here, the African principles known as the *Nguzo Saba* aren't just discussed during Kwanzaa, when each day is a celebration of one of the seven principles, they've become an integral part of all of our work and of families' day-to-day lives.

I work at a family support program in a mostly working class, African American neighborhood. For a long time, my coworkers and I were frustrated with the assessment tools that were available to evaluate the strengths and needs of the families who were coming through our doors. All developed within a Eurocentric paradigm, these tools were inconsistent with the culture we knew and they continued the legacy of allowing others to wrongly define the African American reality.

We decided to start using the Nguzo Saba as the basis of our family assessment process. The Nguzo Saba are seven principles that are the moral and social cement of African cultures: *Umoja* (unity), *Kujichagulia* (self-determination), *Ujima* (collective work and responsibility), *Ujamaa* (cooperative economics), *Nia* (purpose), *Kuumba* (creativity), and *Imani* (faith). For example, when we discuss Umoja with families, we jointly assess the emotional climate of the family, the level of stability and supportiveness, and causes of estrangement. We look for healthy relationships within the family and community. In discussions of Kujichagulia, we talk about family members' motivation, personal and collective empowerment, and interdependence. We look for coercive and oppressive relationships and the silencing of the voices of the vulnerable. We talk about how family members are navigating external systems such as schools, housing, social services, and health care.

The Nguzo Saba resonate with our families. When we engage our families in discussions that are based on these principles, we uncover details about their lives—their extended families, their spirituality, their experiences with racism—that enable us to provide help within a framework that values, supports, and strengthens their cultural identity.

Setting achievable goals is the first step for families seeking to change their situation. Formulating overly ambitious goals may set family members up for failure, thereby further undermining their confidence and effectiveness. Family members become invested, and are most likely to pursue, goals they set for themselves, not goals laid out for them by practitioners.

Some ways to accomplish this are:

● Working with families to identify their strengths, their needs, and the resources that are available to them. Programs may employ a range of formal assessment tools to help with this process. It is important that assessment tools involve parents and be relevant and understandable to them. Practitioners explain to family members the purposes and potential uses of any assessment tool or process. Family members participate in interpreting information gleaned from formal assessment tools. Some programs have developed culturally specific assessment tools which uncover information about identity development, group affiliation, experiences of and responses to discrimination, ties to homeland and/or culture of origin, and relationships to mainstream institutions.

● Working with families to identify strategies and action steps. Practitioners discuss with family members what they want to achieve and then talk with them about possible strategies to pursue. Together they break down large goals into smaller action steps. They discuss available options and likely benefits and consequences of different courses of action. Practitioners encourage families to weigh the priority of one need or goal against that of another. Practitioners listen carefully and clarify and restate the needs and goals that family members embrace.

3

Key Practice 3: Create opportunities for families to gain information and learn new life skills.

When family members acquire new information and develop new skills, they are better able to cope with their lives and to relate positively to their children. For some families this may mean learning basic skills, such as reading and writing. For others, it may mean acquiring a new employment skill. Whatever the case, developing skills enhances family members' ability to function well in their lives and in their child-rearing roles.

Some ways for programs to accomplish this are:

- Offering formal classes, presentations, and workshops. Topics are generated in response to parents' needs and requests and may represent a wide range: basic home and financial management, sewing, gourmet cooking, communication skills, stress reduction, conflict resolution, health issues, arts and crafts, computer skills, GED preparation, English as a second language, and issues for new immigrants. Some programs teach basic skills by setting up "skill stations" at the center in which participants work in small groups. In a mock grocery store, participants can read advertisements and use coupons to shop for a meal they have planned. In the kitchen station, they can prepare and clean up after breakfast. At the bathroom station they learn how to bathe a child safely, how to keep a bathroom clean, and how to help children with tooth-brushing. Other programs will ask a financial advisor to hold a workshop on managing a household budget. Classes and workshops may be facilitated by program staff, volunteers, or program participants.

Practice Example

The family support program helped me believe in myself. I had real low self-esteem; I was a welfare mother and a student and I saw myself as a burden to society. The people in the Parents in Action group would always approach me, and tell me about their potlucks. It took me almost a year to get involved, and gradually, after I started going, I saw that my voice made a difference.

I began to participate more in my daughter's life and I took my nephew in to live with us; he was in a desperate situation and needed help. It's been a real transition in the way I live. Now I'm an advocate for my children, where before I was just more of a caretaker. Now when there's a problem at school, I'll approach a teacher about it. I never would have done that before. And of course, I always speak up at Parents in Action—I learned the skills from them! I used to go to meetings and never say anything except maybe something quiet to the person sitting next to me. I didn't want to offend anyone or go against the grain, I guess. But now, I'll speak up and give my opinions and I'll take action. That's what Parents in Action is for. The leader of the group has really been a mentor for me. I've gone with her to conferences and I've even made presentations.

- Designing the program based on an understanding of how adults learn. Adult family members learn best when they are directly engaged in activities that build on their experiences and strengths, which maximize their participation, and which relate directly to their immediate goals and needs.

- Providing materials in a variety of forms. Programs provide resources in a variety of formats, languages, and media, and at a variety of literacy levels to match families' learning needs with their learning styles and preferences. Many programs provide concrete aids, such as budget sheets, checklists, and picture boards, so that parents can easily apply the information they learn.

- Connecting parents with other places to learn new skills. Programs compile information and provide directories of other local schools, agencies, and service providers that offer skill-building opportunities. Practitioners work with families to increase their ability to access such services and to resolve any difficulties that they may encounter in doing so. Practitioners model effective approaches for other service system employees, and may role-play with parents or even go with them to registration or to a first meeting or appointment with a new service provider.

4

Key Practice 4: Reinforce strengths while families are dealing with challenges or working towards goals.

Problems may be difficult to resolve and progress towards goals occurs neither all at once nor at a consistent pace. Sometimes progress is slow and a number of small steps must be taken and alternative directions must be explored in order to achieve desired outcomes. Programs and practitioners recognize the effort family members make and the sometimes difficult nature of family members' progress. They help families cope with fluctuations in motivation, frustrations with the trial-and-error process, periods of little or no progress, and temporary setbacks. A practitioner's ability to maintain confidence in the family and to consistently emphasize the positive can make the difference between family members giving up or working through stressful times.

Some ways to accomplish this are:

- Helping families focus on the positive. Practitioners discuss family members' progress with them, highlighting steps they've taken and lessons they've learned. During difficult periods, practitioners may review with families the strengths and resources that they initially identified and the families' original sources of motivation. Practitioners may help families tap into additional support by pairing them with other families who have had similar experiences and succeeded.

- Working with the family to adjust their goals, priorities and action plans in response to changes in their needs and interests and the emergence of unforeseen barriers and limitations.

- Acknowledging and celebrating incremental gains. Programs often publicly acknowledge family members' successes by posting their accomplishments on bulletin boards; including them in newsletters; and holding graduations, awards ceremonies, and recognition dinners. Practitioners send personalized note cards or call with encouragement and congratulations. They also encourage families to incorporate acknowledgement and celebration of accomplishments into their family activities.

Practice Example

Patty dropped out of school after eighth grade. Her parents didn't pay attention to her studies and attendance at school. Unfortunately, Patty's school didn't seem to pay much attention either. Teachers passed her from grade to grade without Patty having learned to read and write well.

Patty married in her teens and had two children by the time she was twenty-one. Deeply desiring a good life for her children, Patty recognized a good education as a means to that end. However, her own negative experiences in school and her illiteracy prevented her from promoting her children's education as much as she would have liked.

"When they would come to me with a book and say, 'Read me a story, Mommy,' I would push them away and pretend I was too tired or too busy," Patty said. "But I really didn't want them to know how stupid I was. For the longest time I was afraid that my kids would find out that I couldn't read."

It was this fear that eventually led Patty to confide her secret to Jenny, one of the workers at the family resource center that was located in the school.

Jenny helped Patty enroll in a family literacy program that enabled Patty and her kids to work together to improve their reading skills. She also helped Patty recognize and value all of the other ways in which she was helping to support her children's education—like turning on Sesame Street instead of cartoons for her young son, or volunteering her considerable sewing skills to make costumes for the school play, buying that encyclopedia set one volume at a time from the supermarket, and getting her high school–aged nephew to tutor her daughter, who was having trouble with phonics.

Being able to read has changed Patty's life in many ways, not the least of which is the enjoyable time she now spends reading to her children.

Key Practice 5: Facilitate families' decision to "move on" when the program has met their needs or when they need something that the program does not offer.

Creating dependency is antithetical to the process of building on strengths. Family support programs do not seek to develop reliance on the program, but intentionally promote family members' abilities to master their own lives. In doing so, families learn to access the resources they need, including but not limited to those the program has to offer. When families choose to "move on," but also want to maintain contact, programs facilitate their ongoing involvement and provide opportunities for them to assume new roles.

Some ways to accomplish this are:

● Structuring "exit opportunities." Programs, especially long-term programs, promote the psychological well-being of participants who are ready to move on by designing opportunities for them to do so and rituals or procedures to accompany this transition. These include courses of a specified duration, graduation ceremonies, transition points agreed upon at the beginning of the family's contact with the program (such as when x is achieved, y will happen), and regular evaluation meetings.

● Encouraging the continuation of friendships. Practitioners encourage friendships between families, which will continue after families leave the program. Practitioners view families as "friends of the program" and assure parents that they are always welcome to drop by or come back.

● Providing opportunities for former participants to take part in program activities. Many programs publish newsletters, sponsor events that include the larger community, and host occasional reunions. Former participants may become volunteers for the program, staff members, or participants in alumni groups or advisory councils.

● Making sure that families know about other available resources—such as those offered by libraries, public health departments, schools, and other community institutions like churches— and how to access them.

Guideline D: Programs approach parents as significant resources for each other and for the program.

Key Practice 1: Ensure that parent input shapes all aspects of the program.

Family support programs are designed, implemented, and revised with maximum input from participants, so that the services and activities offered reflect their concerns and interests and meet their needs. When their opinions are solicited and acted upon, family members recognize their value to the program.

Some ways to accomplish this are:

● Including family participants as a sizeable portion, if not the majority, of the program's governance structure. Programs encourage parent participation in meetings by planning them with family members' schedules in mind and by setting and distributing agendas that clearly intend to maximize parents' voices and decision making.

Practice Example

Our family is lucky. When we relocated because of my career in the army, we ended up in a medium-sized city where crime is pretty low and the schools are good. There's a parent-and-child center serving both the base and the general community, where parents can drop in with their kids to meet other families and get relief from the stress that can build up.

We've really depended on the center, so a few years ago when it lost some of its government funding, the other parents and I were worried. The center's staff invited us to a meeting to look at the budget and brainstorm. I was surprised to find that our "little" center has an annual budget of $700,000!

Some parents thought up the idea for a fundraising Halloween party. We invited parents and kids from the whole community to join in bobbing for apples, a costume contest, and games. That first year, we raised $1,000 from the admission charge and sales of raffle tickets. I got use of the recreation center on the base for free, and we spent only $75 on supplies, thanks to businesses that donated food, beverages, and publicity. With that experience under our belts, we saw that we had the potential to do a lot more.

Now the Halloween party has grown into a major source of funding that the center counts on. Parents got co-sponsorship from the Junior League and the YMCA; we hold the party at a large shopping mall that's centrally located and familiar to families (and it makes a great haunted house!). Last year the Halloween party generated $15,000 through corporate and private donations, admission, food and beverage sales, and raffle tickets—and it's totally parent-run. We're upping our goal to $20,000 next year; we want to include a road race and a fun run earlier in the day.

The process of looking at the budget and taking more control of the center's future has been good for everyone. I feel like it's made me a better parent and more active in the community.

● Listening to parents and incorporating their suggestions. Programs incorporate a structured process to ensure that they are developed with parent involvement and reviewed by parents as they are implemented. A governance structure with strong parental representation helps to make sure that this occurs, but parents also need to be involved on committees and work groups that develop and assess programs.

● Creating opportunities for parents and families to design and lead events and activities that meet their needs and enlist their skills.

● Using focus groups, key informant interviews, surveys, and evaluation instruments. These are used both during design of the program and at periodic intervals to ensure that the program remains responsive. Programs make sure that participants are involved in and represented on special committees and in all program initiatives.

● Creating informal mechanisms for participants to make suggestions about the program. Many programs put a suggestion box in a public place, convene meetings for this purpose, or designate a section of a bulletin board or the front of the refrigerator for parents' notes and comments.

Key Practice 2: Facilitate mutually helpful peer-to-peer relationships among program participants.

Family-to-family interaction is a hallmark of family support programs. By forming relationships with each other, families become aware that others are struggling with similar challenges and issues. Family members feel less isolated and overwhelmed. Parents learn from one another and feel increasingly connected and supported. In helping others, family members become more aware of their own strengths.

2

Some ways to accomplish this are:

● Facilitating the flow of information and resources among parents concerning child development and parenting. Programs create mentor programs that pair families with other families; form parent-child play groups; establish bulletin boards, directories, and newsletters that inform parents of resources; form parent-led discussion and support groups; and offer classes and workshops that are run by parents.

● Assisting families in developing skills for assisting and supporting others. Programs provide training and other opportunities for families to improve skills such as in communication, maintaining confidentiality, and problem solving.

- Encouraging exchange and sharing of material resources and services such as childcare, transportation, clothing, toys, and equipment.

- Fostering the continuation of linkages among parents even after they leave the program.

Enhancing Family Capacity: Challenges In Practice

1. Practitioners and program developers sometimes have difficulty viewing parents as resources.

In this society, the traditional belief that each individual is responsible for solving his or her own problems alone makes it difficult to see that those who seek help have strengths and resources to share. Funding for programs that serve families and family members has almost always depended on the identification of deficits in the families to be served or costly problems that could be prevented, not on promoting strength and health of individuals or families. Traditional training of human services professionals focuses primarily on diagnosing and treating problems, not on identifying and building on strengths. Although many factors conspire to prevent those who work with families from viewing those families as resources, a number of strategies for overcoming the deficit model have been used successfully by experienced practitioners and program developers.

First, practitioners and program developers continuously question their assumptions about the families with whom they work. When a family exhibits behaviors that seem problematic to the practitioner, for example, the practitioner asks whether these behaviors could be adaptive responses that the family has used in the past to successfully cope with stressful situations. These behaviors may indicate that the family might benefit from considering alternative strategies for achieving its goals. Perhaps the family can achieve success by taking steps that build on its past experiences. If a family member fails to follow through on plans that have been developed mutually with the practitioner, perhaps it is because in past relationships he or she views as similar to the one being established with the practitioner, his or her competencies were ignored. The program in which the family is participating, or other programs or agencies, may have failed to provide enough opportunities for the family to practice new skills or to take steps that would enable them to develop skills and confidence.

Second, the practitioner, with the support of the program manager, investigates the possibility that he or she may at some level want to maintain power by treating family members as if they have few strengths. When the family is not viewed as resourceful, the practitioner maintains a certain degree of power based on his or her expertise and authority. While it is gratifying to see families display and develop their competencies, the practitioner may also feel uncomfortable with the realization that the family doesn't need her or his expertise anymore.

Third, practitioners need basic knowledge and ongoing learning to engage families effectively as resources. Programs learn what constitutes family strengths from published research on family dynamics and human ecology and on the cultural and community contexts that help define families' strengths and the resources that are available to them. The practitioner who is does not understand the family's culture and background will find it hard to recognize culturally specific strengths.

Finally, an organization that treats staff as resources to the program models and encourages this kind of practice with families. The program's governing body and administration support practitioners so that they can maximize families' resources and contributions. Formal and informal staff development and administrative support emphasize engaging families as resources. Staff members' workloads allow time for the practitioner and the family to build their relationship; this process is necessary if families are to share their strengths and resources.

2. It is often difficult to change staff members' orientation from that of case manager and advocate for families to one that emphasizes empowering families to be their own "case managers" and advocates.

Family support program staff come from a variety of different backgrounds. Some have been case managers in non–family support settings. Some have had extensive training in casework methods and experience as advocates for families in the context of a variety of different agencies and service providers. Some come to family support with a strong commitment to help people or with experience as a community leader who gets things done for others. Utilizing the strengths and skills of staff members and simultaneously offering parents a chance to acquire these same skills can be a challenge for both individual practitioners and programs.

To facilitate staff members' transition from traditional "helping" to empowering, programs provide them with extensive orientation and support, opportunities to learn the new way of working through role playing and feedback, and a program environment in which power is shared and mutual learning is valued. For practitioners, these program characteristics promote the continuous learning that is critical to their success in taking a new approach with families. Practitioners need an opportunity to reflect on their own skills and experiences in being effective "case managers" so that they can be more helpful in assisting parents in acquiring the same skills for themselves.

3. Professionals sometimes refrain from fully sharing their expertise with families in an effort to respect families' abilities and rights.

When practitioners begin taking an approach that is based on strengths and resources, they sometimes become reluctant to share their knowledge and expertise because they want to avoid imposing their ideas and values on families. Sharing expertise in reciprocal, non-hierarchical ways is both a skill and an art. In order to promote the family's development and empowerment, the practitioner maintains a steadfast belief in the family's strengths and capacity. The practitioner defines her or his partnership with the family as one of shared responsibility, equality, and reciprocal exchange. From this perspective, the practitioner has the responsibility to fully share his or her expertise while encouraging and supporting the family's contributions to the partnership. If the practitioner has worked with the family to clearly identify the respective roles and responsibilities of each, then the likelihood of overstepping boundaries is reduced.

During crisis situations in which families experience urgent needs, practitioners respond immediately and apply their knowledge and skills fully. While this response may feel to the family support practitioner like "taking over," this may

be exactly what the family needs and wants in the short term, and the family will feel supported and validated when the practitioner takes a role that matches their needs. In cases in which the safety and well-being of children is threatened, the rights of the children to be protected from harm are the practitioner's first priority; the practitioner responds immediately with all of the resources that are at his or her disposal.

4. Practitioners who are working intensively and individually with families, such as those in home visiting programs, sometimes have difficulty maintaining a balanced focus on the parent-child relationship and may find themselves over-identifying with either the child or with the parent.

Working with the relationship between parent and child is different than working with either the parent or the child. Maintaining focus on this relationship instead of on either one of its members can be a challenge. The child's need for positive, nurturing responses from the parent can seem overwhelming, especially when the parent is unable to provide them due to depression, lack of information, or extreme stress. The practitioner's inclination to meet the child's needs or to find someone else to meet those needs is a natural one. The parent's immediate needs for housing, job skills, or emotional support can seem much more important than the opportunity for him or her to gain new skills in child development.

The practitioner's task is to keep in mind the parent-child relationship while seeing that the needs of each individual are met. This juggling task requires the practitioner to empathize with the parent about the immediate stress that he or she is experiencing, helping the parent to resolve the problem, while also sensitively helping the parent to consider the child's needs. The practitioner can assist the parent in seeing how a situation is affecting his or her child and how the parent's reactions to the situation may affect his or her relationship with the child. The practitioner then can offer the parent realistic alternatives for meeting the child's needs without undermining the parent or making him or her feel inadequate.

ENHANCING FAMILY CAPACITY

5. Families who appear to have few strengths on which to build and many barriers to fulfilling their nurturing role sometimes present great challenges for programs and practitioners.

In every community, there are some families who face extreme stress and present ongoing challenges for programs. One family, for example, might need intensive services for different family members, such as drug abuse treatment or hospitalization for mental illness. Conflicts among members of that family may have escalated into domestic violence or running away. Family members may have been involved with the criminal justice system and spent time away from the family in incarceration. The children may have spent time in foster care. And as a result of all of these factors, the family may be chronically unstable economically and sporadically homeless. The situation may be further compounded by the absence of a supportive social network, and by a lack of job skills and work history among the adults in the family.

Finding strengths on which to build in this kind of a situation can be difficult, but a first step is to establish a respectful relationship between practitioner and family that steadies the family's belief in its ability to work through its difficulties. As the family works with the practitioner to identify and deploy its resources, the practitioner-family relationship itself can become a source of strength for the family. The practitioner's task is to glean from the family's story the experiences of success and feelings of confidence that may have been lost in a sea of negative events, and to assist the family in applying what it learned from those successful events to its current situation.

GUIDELINES FOR FAMILY SUPPORT PRACTICE

Principle Four
Programs affirm and strengthen families' cultural, racial, and linguistic identities and enhance their ability to function in a multicultural society.

Family support programs work in many different ways to assist families in preparing their children to grow up in a society that is increasingly diverse in terms of ethnic backgrounds, cultures, and languages. Children need to develop a positive sense of identity and the ability to appreciate and respect people who are different from themselves. As the prime mediators between children and the environment around them, families play a major role in ensuring that children grow up with these capacities. Families are the primary vehicles through which traditions, values, and languages that are passed from generation to generation. Families' beliefs and attitudes significantly influence how children view both other people who are different from them and those who are like them.

In a diverse society such as ours, families' and family members' identities are influenced by numerous forces, which include culture. While it is a truism that people's beliefs and attitudes are developed within and shaped by culture, the ways in which this development and shaping occur are complicated. The boundaries of cultures are not always clear, and there is a great deal of diversity in attitudes, beliefs, and practices within cultures. For example, although Mexican, Puerto Rican, and Cuban Americans may all speak Spanish and be viewed by many as members of the same group (Latino), each has had a very different history, a different experience in the United States, and different cultural practices. Even the Spanish they speak may reflect variations in dialect, vocabulary and meaning of words, and language itself.

Another point to consider is that culture is not the only difference that matters; it is not the only important group affiliation or determinant of an individual's identity. Factors such as class, gender, religion, health status, and sexual orientation all contribute to the formation of identity. And cultural identity itself can be multifaceted: many people partici-

pate in—and consider themselves part of—several different cultures. For example, of what culture is a person born to a Palestinian father and a Colombian mother who was born in and spent his childhood years in Puerto Rico and emigrated to America at age sixteen? If he marries a Polish American woman, of what culture are their children?

In their work with families, programs maintain constant awareness that a child's experience of his or her own identity as part of a culture or race is dramatically impacted by the treatment that group has received and currently receives from the larger society. In the United States, American culture is widely thought to be an amalgam of many different

What Is Culture?[1]

The term "culture" describes the integrated pattern of human behavior that includes actions, assumptions, values, reasoning, and communication of a racial, ethnic, religious, or social group; the combination of thoughts, feelings, attitudes, material traits, and behaviors of a group of people. Each of these characteristics is manifested and shared by the group through symbols and communication and social patterns. Culture is the way that groups interact with their environment to satisfy human needs that we all share. There are many different cultures which reflect many different ways of meeting the same human needs. Culture is a complex system of learned and conditioned responses, and it is therefore one of the greatest resources for helping family support workers understand family needs and strengths.

Culture is not genetic; it is learned through social interaction.

Cultures are dynamic; they change over time and in response to collective experience. Cultures change as a result of how the group is treated (positively or negatively) within the larger society and the exposure of that group to other cultures. The cultural traditions, beliefs, and practices of a family reflect the values and customs of the different groups of which they are members. Some aspects of culture, such as ethnic clothes, foods, and traditional celebrations, may seem like very obvious manifestations. Other aspects, such as the way culture shapes values, world perspectives, and patterns of human interaction, such as how people show respect, are much more subtle.

cultures that have interacted over time, a beautiful crazy quilt, a melting pot. On the other hand, we know that systematic and widespread discrimination against and oppression of certain groups have been present throughout the history of the United States, and have increased and decreased, fluctuating in their persistence and who has been targeted, thereby affecting different generations differently. The United States bears the scars of policies which have ravaged the languages and cultures of certain groups and caused physical and emotional suffering and even death of these groups' members. The long and painful history of the enslavement of African Americans and the placement of Native American children into boarding schools where they were forced to learn the behaviors and manners of the dominant culture are just two examples. Slavery of Africans, which gave way to segregation and Jim Crow laws; genocide of Native Americans; and incarceration of Japanese Americans during World War II are the most blatant examples of past oppression that was governmentally sanctioned. Racist, discriminatory, and biased attitudes and acts persist. One has only to ask and to listen. The formation of one's own cultural identity, and how one experiences that identity, are affected by how members of one's culture are treated by others in society.

All families need skills in preparing their children and themselves to negotiate the increasingly diverse society in which we live. Even if children grow up in seemingly monocultural communities, they are likely to encounter people different from themselves as they travel or move to other parts of the country and as people of different cultures enter their communities. Given current immigration patterns, even traditionally single-ethnic communities are likely to experience some shifts in ethnic composition. Fostering in the next generation the ability to draw strength from diversity is a responsibility that all families, communities, and programs share.

Issues of racial, linguistic, and cultural diversity are addressed throughout this book and have been incorporated into virtually every chapter. This chapter represents only some aspects of effectively addressing issues of diversity; it cannot summarize the many ways in which diversity is discussed throughout the book and is honored by family support programs each day.

When Strengthening Cultural, Racial, and Linguistic Identity Is a Priority

It is the prerogative of families to determine their cultural affiliations and the priority of those affiliations in their lives. Just as a family support staff member does not define who constitutes a participant's family, family support programs don't assume families' membership in a particular culture. Family support programs encourage families to identify their own cultural, linguistic, and racial identities.

Affirming and strengthening cultural, linguistic, and racial identity means different things to different families; it is an important focus to some, but not necessarily all. For example, families who have recently immigrated to the United States, parents who want their children to have strong cultural identities, and members of socially vulnerable, traditionally oppressed groups often seek assistance from family support programs in affirming and strengthening their children's cultural, racial, and linguistic identities. Family support programs help families to affirm and pass on their cultures and languages to their children and counter the effects of racist and otherwise negative messages.

Passing On Cultures and Languages to Children

Families' ability to pass on their cultures and languages supports the well-being of their children and the development of strong bonds among family members. It helps children develop connections to their families and communities and sustain these connections later in life. Many cultural attributes, especially those which are most subtle, are acquired subconsciously as a child is being raised among family and community members.[2]

Language usually is the vehicle by which the community transmits customs and beliefs to children, and therefore, it also is critical that families pass their languages on to their children. Specific community values, beliefs, and traditions are often embedded in particular words and expressions. In many languages, for example, specific words are used to address relatives and respected individuals within the community. Learning these words teaches a child fundamental concepts about the importance of family and respect for elders. Most languages have at least a few words which cannot be meaningfully translated into other languages due to their cultural nuance.

In addition, children whose parents' native language is not English, and who do not learn and maintain their families' first or home languages can experience barriers in their ability to relate to their families. Losing the home language when learning a new one also can impede children's cognitive development at certain stages. Children learn certain concepts (for example, what a number is) best in their home language. If they are struggling to learn such concepts and at the same time a new language, they may not fully grasp them. Studies also show that first developing literacy skills in a language other than English when that language is a family's home language can make it easier for children to learn English.[3]

Even when language-minority parents are highly motivated to learn English, their opportunities to do so are often much more limited than their children's are. Classes in English as a second language classes for adults often are overcrowded, limited in number, and difficult to enter due to long waiting lists. Many meet during the day, which excludes many working parents, and do not offer childcare, which often excludes parents of young children. Adults who do not speak English generally must take jobs that do not call for special skills and do not pay well; these adults, some of whom are undocumented workers, have no choice but to accept jobs for which they are overqualified. The "right" conditions for learning English rarely exist for language-minority parents. Consequently, these parents find that they can no longer engage in meaningful conversations with their children after the children have lost their home language. Parents lose their ability to provide verbal comfort and support, offer guidance and discipline, and transmit their values, hopes, and traditions.[4]

Many native English-speaking Americans are unaware of their own cultural and linguistic roots and welcome opportunities to learn about these roots. When family support programs assist families in learning about their linguistic and cultural history, they foster these families' understanding of who they are. This can be an important activity for adults as well as children and often can be a meaningful shared experience.

How Negative Societal Messages Impact Families

Many families, particularly those who belong to so-called racial minorities[5], face significant challenges as they attempt to pass on to their children a positive sense of their own cultural and linguistic identities and heritage. People often unintentionally and, in some cases, intentionally send the message that those who are not light-complected, who have a cultural background that is other than Western European Christian, or who speak a language other than English are inferior. As the sign in many pediatricians' offices reads: "Children learn what they live." Children respond to the verbal and non-verbal cues in their environment. For example, a child whose parents speak Black English, also known as Ebonics[6], or an Appalachian dialect and are treated disrespectfully or as if they were stupid by teachers, doctors, or other authority figures will observe and may react to that treatment by internalizing these feelings and behaving in a way that fulfills the negative expectations of others. Children notice when their cultural traditions, beliefs, and behaviors are not valued or considered part of the norm. They notice when their families' or communities' lifestyles and day-to-day experiences are marginalized in, absent from, or misrepresented in school, on television, and in stores and public institutions. For example, ask any child of a Muslim, Jewish, Hindu, or Buddhist family how he or she feels at Christmas time. Children take to heart the stereotypical and negative television portrayals of people who bear their image and question their worth when there are no images of their cultural group at all. They learn all too quickly the derogatory terms used by others to refer to people from their ethnic backgrounds. Ashamed of their culture, home language, or skin color, they can begin to reject the very core of their identity. They can become alienated from their families, friends, and communities.

Alternatively, those children or groups who are portrayed as the norm and are reflected positively in a myriad of contexts, including the media, school curricula, toys, games, and books, often have to later confront a false sense of superiority and unlearn many myths about themselves and others. They may also have to contend with the loss that is associated with a lack of exposure to and interaction with others different from themselves.

Ultimately, acting to change these negative messages and to help families develop strategies to deal with them is acting in the interest of all children. Even children who are not members of a group which has been negatively portrayed are affected by what they see and experience. Unless they learn accepting and positive attitudes and receive accurate information about diversity, they will play a part in perpetuating prejudice and discrimination, and will be separated from others in their communities.

Appreciating and Respecting Differences

Enhancing families' ability to function in a culturally diverse society involves assisting families in appreciating and respecting those who are different from themselves. This process begins with developing awareness of what culture is and how it functions in one's own life. It is normal for a person to be centered in his or her own culture and to reflect that culture's attitudes, beliefs, assumptions, and practices without being aware that he or she is doing so. Most people cannot explain their behaviors and outlooks—they just do what feels right and what they conceive of as normal and expected. This lack of awareness exists for people of all cultural groups. In the United States, the people who are least cognizant that their behaviors are embedded in their culture are those whose behaviors are typically deemed "normal" by the media and public institutions; in fact, these people themselves often are represented and experience themselves as the norm. People are uncomfortable with what is unfamiliar or different. In this society there is a prevalent attitude that something is wrong when a person or group approaches a situation in a way that deviates from the norm. Not only are such behaviors considered different; they are considered inferior.

Enhancing families' ability to change these patterns and function in a multicultural society requires operating outside of what is for most people the normal way of going about life. Family support programs offer contexts in which the process of in-depth learning about one's own culture is encouraged. Cultural self-awareness is not just knowing about the dress, food, and holiday celebrations that are specific to one's culture; it is not even enough to know the history, language, communication patterns, and values of that culture. Being aware of and in touch with one's own culture also involves examining its inconsistencies and the aspects of it that might result in conflicts with others over values. It involves taking a close look at how one's cultural background has shaped one's world perspective, beliefs, and behaviors so that a person does not assume that what he or she does or thinks necessarily applies to someone from a different background or experience. It is important to acknowledge that many different strategies exist for addressing any issue, challenge, or need. A thorough understanding of one's own culture is an important foundation for learning about, relating to, and being open to others—including people of different backgrounds. This is as true for program staff as it is for families.

In addition to increasing families' awareness of their own culture programs help families to appreciate and respect people who are different by providing contexts in which people can learn about other cultures and by providing families of different backgrounds opportunities to interact with each other.

Despite the overall cultural and ethnic diversity of this country, racial and economic segregation continues to be pervasive in neighborhoods, schools, and in places of work. As a result, people from different backgrounds do not often get to interact with each other, to get to know each other on a more familiar or meaningful level, much less to establish genuine bonds of kindredness. Family support programs can help to change these patterns.

For example, consider the experience of a family support effort which offered a program where mothers and daughters shared what it meant to grow up and what it meant to be an adolescent. The program involved a wide array of mothers and daughters from different racial as well as class backgrounds. The discussions among the group revealed that many of the hardships and joys involved in weathering adolescence were the same for mothers and daughters regardless of their backgrounds. These types of situations can also allow people from different backgrounds to gain a better understanding of their differences. Affluent mothers, for instance, can become more aware of barriers faced by poor mothers in the group, such as the lack of recreational opportunities or the absence of jobs which pay a living wage. Such types of program can help both groups to question their stereotypes because it encourages them to listen to each other's personal stories and situations. Finally, this setting can create an opportunity for groups to identify issues which cannot be addressed unless families work together across boundaries of race, language, socio-economic class, and culture to change the situation. Family support practitioners act on the knowledge that in order to both develop their own voices and build their sense of community, families may need to have access to both mono-ethnic and multi-ethnic activities.

Understanding and Negotiating the Dominant Culture

For many families—including those who have recently come to the U.S., those who speak a language other than English at home, or families whose cultural background is different from that of the mainstream or who have moved to a community that is very different from the one in which they were raised—enhancing the ability to function in a multicultural society involves understanding and negotiating the dominant U.S. culture and language. Programs can help parents obtain accurate information about the norms and practices of U.S. institutions. For example, different cultures have very different views about how to appropriately discipline a child and the degree to which corporal punishment is acceptable. Many families do not understand what constitutes child abuse and neglect in the U.S. or what rights they have as parents. They are unfamiliar with the institution of child protective services. They do not have reliable information about how particular agencies or systems operate or what the applicable rules or policies are. This lack of understanding may result in unnecessary conflict or distress. Parents may become afraid to discipline their children in any fashion and as a result find themselves at a loss about how to maintain control.

Programs can also introduce families to the U.S. norms regarding advocacy and democracy. Introducing families to voting, petitioning, and the belief in the right of families to advocate on their own behalf can equip families to participate in shaping institutions and policies which are in keeping with their beliefs and values. Programs can also work with public institutions and social service agencies in their communities to help them learn about and become more responsive to people of different cultural backgrounds. These processes further mutual sharing and understanding, and an increased awareness of and respect for cultural differences.

NOTES

[1] Cross, T. (1996) "Developing a knowledge base to support cultural competence." *FRC Report* 14 (3–4) 4.

[2] Chang, H., D. Pulido Tobiassen, and A. Muckelroy (In press) *Looking in, looking out: Redefining early care and education in a diverse society.* (San Francisco, Calif.: California Tomorrow).

[3] Cummins, J. (1989) *Empowering minority students.* (Sacramento, Calif.: California Association for Bilingual Education).

[4] Wong Fillmore, L. (1991) "When learning a second language means losing the first." *Early Childhood Research Quarterly* 6.

Chang, H. and L. Sakai (1993) *Affirming children's roots: Cultural and linguistic diversity in early child care and education.* (San Francisco, Calif.: California Tomorrow).

[5] Groups commonly referred to as "minorities" are in fact the majority in many regions of the United States, including some of the nation's largest cities. In Chicago, for example, 52.8 percent of the city's population is African American, Native American/Eskimo, Asian/Pacific Islander, or of another non-white ethnic background. [Chicago Department of Planning and Development (1994) *Demographic characteristics of Chicago's population.* (Chicago, Ill.)]

In California, one of the nation's largest states, since 1987 the percentage of school-age children who are members of the so-called minority groups (Asian, Pacific Islander, Filipino, Hispanic, African American, and American Indian/Alaskan Native) has consistently increased. As of 1995, these children constituted 59.6 percent of the total school population. [California Department of Education (1996) *1995–1996 Fact Book: Handbook of education information.* (Sacramento, Calif.)]

[6] There is an increasing number of individuals who advocate that Black English is a legitimate dialect, with specific patterns and a standard set of grammatical rules, which should be recognized as such. Among this group, the preferred term for Black English is Ebonics.

Affirming Diversity: Guidelines for Practice

Some family support programs are located in culturally homogeneous neighborhoods and therefore serve families of a single cultural group; others are multicultural. All family support programs affirm participants' cultural, ethnic, racial, and linguistic identity; promote cross-cultural understanding and respect for differences; and help families navigate the dominant U.S society and culture—even as they work to make society more supportive of all families.

Guidelines and Key Practices

Guideline A: Programs support and affirm expressions of cultural and linguistic identity.
Key Practices
1. Build upon the cultural beliefs and practices of the families and communities the program serves.
2. Help families pass on their cultures and languages to their children.
3. Foster opportunities for families of the same ethnic or cultural group to spend time together.

Guideline B: Programs work with families to combat racist attitudes (and other attitudes that promote hate) and to promote the development of positive cultural, ethnic, and racial identities among children.
Key Practices
1. Create an environment that reflects positive images of different cultural, ethnic, and racial groups and does not portray anyone negatively.
2. Create opportunities for staff and adult family members to become more aware of actions, beliefs, or words that may promote bias.
3. Assist parents in understanding their role as mediators of their children's experiences and support them in this role.
4. Identify and challenge institutional forms of discrimination.

Guideline C: Programs strengthen staff and families' ability to relate to those who are different from themselves.
Key Practices
1. Create an environment of continuous learning about cultures—one's own and others.
2. Create opportunities for families of different backgrounds to identify areas of common ground and to accept and value differences between them.

Guideline D: Programs help families to understand and negotiate the dominant culture and language of the United States.
Key Practices
1. Serve as a resource for information on how the dominant U.S. culture and institutions function, and how national, state, and local policies affect children and families.
2. Teach the skills parents and staff need in order to work with, participate in, and advocate within institutions and agencies in this society.
3. Work with other community agencies and service providers to increase their understanding of and ability to relate to families of different cultural backgrounds.

Guideline E: Hiring policies and training opportunities reflect the program's priority on affirming diversity.
Key Practices
1. Include staff who reflect the cultural and ethnic experiences and languages of the families with whom they work and integrate their expertise into the entire program.
2. Provide ongoing staff development on the issues that diversity presents.

Guideline A: Programs support and affirm expressions of cultural and linguistic identity.

Key Practice 1: Build upon the cultural beliefs and practices of the families and communities the program serves.

Family support programs find ways to ensure that their environments, activities, staff, and ways of delivering services are all congruent with the values, beliefs, and practices of the families who participate. This congruence is necessary for the programs to fulfill the goal of affirming cultural, linguistic, and racial identities. In multicultural communities, programs build on the beliefs and practices of the different cultures represented in order to affirm the identities of all groups. Activities may be carried out in a way that consciously affirms one group and provides a learning opportunity for another.

Some ways to accomplish this are:

● Encouraging practitioners to learn about the cultures of the families and communities with which they interact. A practitioner learns about a culture by spending time with strong, healthy people of that culture; finding a "cultural guide" (i.e., someone from the culture who is willing to discuss the culture, introduce the practitioner to experiences that are new to him or her, and help him or her to understand those experiences); reading widely, including articles by and for persons of the culture, professional literature, and fiction; attending cultural events and meetings of leaders from within the culture; and learning how to ask questions in sensitive ways. Practitioners also may want to invest time in learning the languages of program participants.

● Fostering and encouraging dialogue about culture. Practitioners explore with families their values, ideas about child rearing, and beliefs and cultural practices. Practitioners help families to identify and articulate values and practices that are important to them. Programs encourage families and staff to share information informally and to ask each other questions about their respective heritages. Programs encourage families to talk to staff if they feel they do not understand the practices of the program or feel that these practices are inconsistent with what they do at home.

Practice Example

In my first month at the family resource center, I facilitated a group for parents of first-graders. Sometimes it's hard to encourage parents to help each other when they have problems while showing respect for different styles of parenting. One evening the group was talking about the challenges of helping their children learn to write. Mr. Petrazinski said his son kept getting frustrated when he couldn't fit his writing onto the big lines in his notebook. He'd erase and erase until there were holes in the paper, get upset, and often go into a temper tantrum.

Ms. Lee said that when her mother was raising her in Hong Kong, she never would have "let her child go" like that. She would sit by her for hours, and taught her to write by holding her hand as she herself stroked the characters onto the page with her calligraphy pen. Ms. Lee said Mr. Petrazinski needed to be patient with his son, not to scare him, and to help him a little more.

I could see the veins popping out in Mr. Petrazinski's neck. I asked him why he thought it was important to let his child solve his own problems. "I want to help!" he said. "But I want him to have a chance to make mistakes." Mr. Petrazinski said his mother had watched him so closely as a child that he felt he never got to learn things for himself. He wanted something better for his son. As he talked on, he also realized he was uncomfortable holding onto his child's hand. A recently divorced father, he was participating in child-rearing for the first time.

I asked Ms. Lee what she would suggest Mr. Petrazinski do. She thought for a long moment. Then she suggested that he set up "formal time for informal writing practice." "Give him paper without lines," she suggested. "Let him ask you how to spell words and then write them whatever size he wants, anywhere on the page. But when it's time to do his penmanship homework, try holding his hand just for one word at the beginning of each sentence. And be patient."

"I guess it's like training wheels!" said Mr. Petrazinski. "You help him get started, then let him go."

● Designing program components so that they address cultural needs and incorporate cultural values. Programs translate program materials into languages used by program participants. Programs also prepare materials that can be easily understood by families with limited literacy skills in their native language.

● Celebrating holidays and special events incorporating educational and artistic activities. Families participate in planning and orchestrating these events so that they reflect families' values and accurately express their cultures. Programs use these and other activities as opportunities for families to share cultural expressions with each other.

Key Practice 2: Help families pass on their cultures and languages to their children.

Programs recognize the importance of maintaining culture and language to affirming parents' cultural and linguistic identities. The primary way to maintain and preserve culture is through socialization, that is passing the language, beliefs, and practices on to children. When programs provide a supportive environment for this process and when they act as partners with parents in their efforts to teach and raise their children in a culturally appropriate manner, parents and children feel that their culture is valued.

Some ways to accomplish this are:

● Creating opportunities for adult members of families that participate in the program and other adults in the community to teach children and each other about the beliefs, traditions and history of the group.

● Providing staff with information on how children develop a sense of cultural, ethnic, and linguistic identity.

● Creating opportunities for family and community members to rediscover, reclaim, and recreate traditions, beliefs, languages, and family history. For example, many Native American tribes are trying to preserve their languages by teaching children and youth how to speak them even if their parents do not. Many programs in African American communities organize themselves around the Nguzo Saba (seven principles articulated as the basis of African culture by Maulana Karenga in the 1960s, see Practice Example on page 37). One program in San Francisco sponsors Chinese American children's trips to China to find and document their family roots.

● Incorporating the values, beliefs, traditions, symbols, idioms, and language(s) of all cultures served by the program into all activities.

● Helping families recognize and negotiate threats to their ability to maintain their cultures and languages and pass them on to their children.

Key Practice 3: Foster opportunities for families of the same ethnic or cultural group to spend time together.

Family support programs provide contexts where people of the same cultural, linguistic, or ethnic group get together to speak to others in their native language, to identify and share their common needs and experiences, and to identify their shared interests. Being with members of one's

2

3

own ethnic or cultural group is affirming. It also allows an individual to understand how his or her experience may or may not be common to a larger group experience. When people who have confronted racism or prejudice don't know that others in their group have suffered the same experiences, it is easy for them to attribute the problem to their own personal deficiencies rather than to larger social and political issues. Spending time together can help people become more aware of how they can take positive steps towards improving their individual lives and the well-being of the group as a whole. These contexts also help people of groups that have been discriminated against and oppressed to recognize and work through internalized oppression. When people talk to and meet members of their groups who have succeeded, they realize that they can take positive steps to change their destiny even in the face of the discrimination and inequities that exist. Families who are part of or who represent the dominant culture may also find it beneficial to get together to explore ways to interrupt prejudicial, stereotypical, and discriminatory behaviors and beliefs—and to discuss the cost of maintaining such behaviors to their community and to society.

Some ways for programs to accomplish this are:

Practice Example

My best friend Aaron and I always go to Mr. Johnson when something's going on with us. He's our leader in the Brother-to-Brother program at the Dr. Martin Luther King, Jr. Center. It's right in the project.

A year ago we got hassled by the police while we were just buying some soda in the store. It was the third time that month, and we were sick of it. But you always have to just be cool and respectful, otherwise they hassle you even more. But me and Aaron were fed up. So we went to Mr. Johnson.

Next thing, he's asking us to lead a discussion on police harassment with the rest of our Brother-to-Brother group—and some of the Black police officers from the community! We were both nervous—you know, we'd never done something like that. But he got us started by asking us just to talk about what happened to us at the store that day, and what we thought was wrong with how we were treated. We got the whole group talking about the problem.

The police officers mostly listened. Then one of them said he respected us for having the courage to lead this group. He said the store owners deserved protection from gang-bangers and kids who steal, but that we deserved to not be hassled just because we're young and Black.

Now Aaron and myself are on a city-wide board where we represent youth in our project—we sit right next to the police officers, aldermen, and business owners. Aaron thought up an idea and told it to one of the store owners, and she's using it. She's mentoring some kids—teaching them about running a business, in exchange for some help around the store. We're working on other solutions. We're trying to get more Brother-to-Brother programs, because part of it is that too many kids are out on the street. Me and Aaron know, because we've been there.

- Creating safe space where families of similar culture and background can gather together and find community, support, and cultural and emotional sustenance.

- Creating a program environment that reflects the cultural style of the program's participants.

- Hiring staff that reflect the participants' culture and background and providing ongoing staff development opportunities in group facilitation.

- Providing activities that are planned by and designed for members of a specific cultural group.

B

1

Guideline B: Programs work with families to combat racist attitudes (and other attitudes that promote hate) and to promote the development of positive cultural, ethnic, and racial identities among children.

Key Practice 1: Create an environment that reflects positive images of different cultural, ethnic, and racial groups and does not portray anyone negatively.
An essential part of both developing positive identity and improving the ability of people from

different backgrounds to appreciate and respect each other is creating contexts in which differences are recognized, affirmed, and valued. Programs seek to create an environment which celebrates diversity and discourages bias and stereotyping. In this way, they inherently combat racism and contribute to the development of positive cultural, racial, and ethnic identities in all of their participants.

Some ways for programs to accomplish this are:

- Making sure that the program's decor contains positive images of people of different cultural, ethnic, and racial backgrounds. Programs pay attention to the details, incorporating cultural elements wherever possible. Programs post culturally appropriate artwork and posters on the walls; have diverse toys and storybooks in the childcare areas; make sure that fabrics used for tablecloths and furniture, dishes, implements for communal meals, musical instruments, and other objects used in program activities reflect the cultures of the families served.

- Reviewing all program materials, including books, videos, and curricula, to ensure that they don't project negative attitudes toward specific cultural or ethnic groups or toward diversity, and that they incorporate authentic information about diverse groups.

- Modeling respectful relationships. Program staff do not espouse or tolerate derogatory comments or ethnic slurs.

- Supporting staff in identifying elements of bias and prejudice and how this relates to institutional discrimination, such as racism.

Practice Example

I grew up on this farm, and now I'm raising my kids here. It's hard sometimes—the girls ride the bus an hour just to get to the school in the nearby city, but in a way it's good, because they meet people who are different.

There's a program through the school that gets kids and their parents involved in activities together. They even have a van that drops them off afterward, so those of us who live out here can go, too. This winter, when things slowed down here and I had some time on my hands, I went with the girls and some other kids and parents to the Holocaust exhibit at a museum in the city. I held my girls' hands while we walked through it, guided by a recording of a little Jewish boy telling about how his family had gotten thrown out of their house in Poland. We entered a room set up like a train car, and the boy's voice said this was how they got transported to the concentration camp. Then we walked on to a bare room, set up with some dingy bunks. This was the room the boy lived in, with hardly any food, no heat, packed in with other people and separated from his parents.

At the end we all sat down together and tried to figure out what it all meant—the group leader handed out some questions, like, "Could this ever happen again?" and "If it did, what would you do?" We talked about how some people still think other people aren't really people, just because they're different. My girls chimed in and said they didn't believe that. They said all people were naturally different.

When I was a kid, everyone I knew was like me. When a new kid moved into the area, life was hard for him if his daddy was poor—let alone if he was from a different country or was a different color. I'm proud of my kids. I've even learned from them!

Key Practice 2: Create opportunities for staff and adult family members to become more aware of actions, beliefs, and words that may promote bias.

Eliminating racist and hate-promoting attitudes from the program's environment requires commitment on the part of staff and families. It is not enough to have good intentions; well-meaning people contribute to stereotyping and bias in inadvertent and subtle ways. All of us are born into a world in which stereotypes exist. They are manifested in aspects of the cultures of which we are a part and are endorsed by the institutions that we respect and trust (e.g., the media, schools, religious institutions, families, and communities). Programs help staff and families conscientiously develop sensitivity to and awareness of both subtle and overt manifestations of bias, prejudice, and stereotyping, and facilitate communication that will help to eliminate them.

Some ways to accomplish this are:

2

3

Practice Example

When the snow starts to melt, my two girls demand that their father and I take them to the park to start practicing for Little League softball. And my teenaged son, Nassir, is a budding track star. They must have gotten their athletic genes from their father.

While we're happy that they're so enthusiastic about athletics, we see the softball and basketball seasons approaching with some trepidation. Last year was our first in the United States, and there were heated arguments between us and the kids over whether Nassir could compete over Diwali (it is the most important holiday of the year, and unfortunately, it's in November, when his school's invitational cross-country meet is) and what our kids would eat after the game, since hot dogs seem to be such a big part of the softball game festivities. We are strict vegetarians and do not eat any meat. I know it hurts them when they are made to feel different. But why does it have to be one or the other? Why can't they be Hindu and American?

These questions came up again this year, and I decided to talk with the woman who looks after my daughters after school. There's a family resource center attached to the school that supervises children of working parents from three to five o'clock. She said she knew a teacher in our school system who was from India and would probably be willing to sit down to brainstorm with the coaches and me.

The teacher, the coaches, and I came up with some great ideas. The softball coach would arrange to have vegetarian "hot dogs" at the games, and a brand new pot to cook them in that would be kept separately and never come into any contact with any meat. It gave them a good excuse to provide a no-cholesterol alternative for the other parents! And Nassir's coach, once she knew when Diwali fell, said she'd plan the meet for a week earlier in November.

I feel good about teaching our children that the Hindu and the American parts of their identities don't have to be at war with each other. There are more and more Indian families moving into our school district, so I hope what I did gives other parents courage and pride. Perhaps we can also broaden the perspective of the Christian kids as well.

● Creating an environment in which people are supported when they raise questions. Programs establish guidelines for communicating about cultural and social differences in order to help create a safe, supportive environment. Programs develop and teach skills that participants and staff can use to mediate and resolve conflicts.

● Promoting communication about feelings. Families and staff examine together their cultural biases, prejudices, and stereotypes and discuss these topics and their feelings about them. Programs provide supportive contexts and foster ways that staff and families can constructively discuss incidents where one person perceives that another has made an offensive comment or behaved in a discriminatory or unjust manner.

● Incorporating an anti-bias curriculum for children into the program.

● Reviewing program policies with all staff and families.

● Working with families to develop strategies for intervening and interacting with children so that they develop positive cultural, ethnic, and racial identities and unbiased attitudes towards other.

Key Practice 3:   Assist parents in understanding their role as mediators of their children's experiences and support them in this role.

Part of a parent's role is to help his or her children articulate, interpret, and make sense of their experiences—especially troubling and difficult experiences—and to develop adaptive strategies for dealing with them. Unfortunately, for many families this means negotiating in very pragmatic ways encounters with hate-promoting attitudes and racist practices. Family support programs bolster parents' efforts to maintain their children's positive identities. Programs reinforce parents' efforts to teach their children how to manage relationships, maintain a strong self-image, and achieve their goals in environments that can be hostile.

Some ways to accomplish this are:

● Using classes and workshops on issues related to parenting as forums to discuss strategies for confronting and addressing prejudice and discriminatory behavior or attitudes.

4

Parents may share their feelings and discuss their approaches for helping their children deal with situations in which they are discriminated against or made to feel badly about others' or their cultures or ethnic identities.

● Using parent-child interaction as opportunities to bring to the surface issues that children are facing as they attempt to maintain their cultural identities when they are in the minority. Practitioners use role-playing with both children and adults.

● Fostering in parents the feeling that they are entitled to a society that is responsive to and inclusive of their cultural needs and helping them become assertive in requiring that those needs be met. Programs help families identify situations that they would like to change and develop skills and strategies for changing them.

● Helping parents advocate on behalf of their children and their communities.

Key Practice 4: Identify and challenge institutional forms of discrimination.

Family support programs understand that racism and other types of discrimination are built into many of the institutions of this society. Discrimination impairs families' abilities to affirm their cultural, linguistic, and racial identities and to achieve what they would like for their own and for their children's fulfillment. Family support programs therefore join forces with parents and communities to recognize discriminatory policies and practices and to work to abolish them.

Some ways to accomplish this are:

● Creating a policy for resolution of disputes within the program.

● Forming partnerships with other community organizations that want to create anti-oppressive and affirming environments. These collaborations may sponsor community forums to promote dialogue on cultural differences and explore social justice issues.

● Working with families and groups of families to identify barriers that they face and to discuss ways of overcoming them. Family support program staff work with families to develop strategies for changing discriminatory situations or

Practice Example

Most parents in our program came to this country from Mexico and are working in low-paying service jobs. They want a better life for their children. I remember one father, Mr. Garcia, who wanted desperately for his son, Marcos, to do well in school. "I make him study all evening," said Mr. Garcia. "No TV, no girl-friends—but still, he fails." I asked what courses he was taking, and Mr. Garcia named a lot of vocational classes like shop, but nothing that would prepare him for college.

One of our bilingual staff members, Marta, used to be a guidance counselor. With Mr. Garcia's permission, I set up a meeting between her and Marcos, to see what we could do. Marcos confided to her that he was really bored in school. He wanted to be a doctor, not a mechanic—but his teachers had steered him away from chemistry and physics. Marta visited Mr. Garcia and suggested that Marcos take a placement test to see what science class he'd fit into. The next semester, Marcos was taking chemistry (and doing great!). He was trading Spanish tutoring for science tutoring with another student, to catch up on the previous semester's work.

The problem of tracking in the school system wasn't limited to Marcos; his experience was typical of Mexican American kids. Other parents were frustrated that their children weren't getting enough out of school and weren't going to go to college.

Marta and I asked Mr. Garcia if he wanted to work with some other parents to make their voices heard. He said yes. He invited some other parents who were friends of his to meet at the family center to talk about their concerns. The same themes came up: bright kids who wanted to learn, but needed to be told they could succeed in college. Teachers who seemed to assume that Spanish-speaking children weren't as smart or as capable as their Anglo counterparts. Parents who cared so much about their children, were angry that they were being underestimated, and felt powerless and intimidated by the school system.

Marta and I told the parents about the PTA, and told them we'd support them if they wanted to join and advocate for their children's education. They joined as a group. Now they make up one-fourth of the PTA—enough to make a real presence. They've made a short-term list of proposals, like getting a bilingual guidance counselor into the school, along with long-range goals, like documenting the school's tracking problem officially and getting the state department of education to do something about it.

AFFIRMING DIVERSITY

prevailing in these situations and for helping families to make their community institutions more responsive to their needs. A family support program could, for example, work with families to advocate for a multicultural curriculum in their local school or to launch a letter-writing campaign aimed at the local media.

- Encouraging staff to name and interrupt program practices and community and institutional norms that are discriminatory or inequitable.

Guideline C: Programs strengthen staff and families' ability to relate to those who are different from themselves.

Key Practice 1: Create an environment of continuous learning about cultures—one's own and others.

Those in the field of family support envision a multicultural society that consistently recognizes, values, and celebrates cultural differences, and a society whose members live the ideal of democracy by accepting all cultures. In order to get there, we all have a lot of learning to do. It is essential to gain an awareness of the way in which our culture has shaped our experience of the world. This self-awareness provides a foundation for learning about others. Gaining insight into other cultures promotes respect for and appreciation of differences and enhances people's ability to function effectively in a multicultural society.

Some ways for programs to accomplish this are:

- Encouraging families and staff to develop self-awareness. Programs encourage participants and staff to delve deeply into their own cultures and to learn not only about traditional forms of dress, foods, holiday celebrations, history, language, communication patterns, and values, but also about the biases and assumptions about other cultures that they have internalized, and about areas in which their cultures conflict with others.

- Providing workshops, classes, and forums that inform staff and participants about diverse cultures and social groups that reside within their community and the larger society.

- Fostering a nurturing environment that promotes dialogue and supports communication around diversity issues, with an expectation that conflicts and misunderstandings may arise. When conflicts or misunderstandings surface, they are viewed as opportunities for learning, and therefore not feared or suppressed.

Practice Example

What you in America call "coining,' and we call Cao Giao, is a traditional way of healing in Vietnam. When my grandson got sick last spring, we knew the only way he would get better was through this time-honored method.

Thank goodness he got better, and went back to school. But after he got home that first day, a stranger came to our apartment and said she was from the department of child protection (I had no idea what that was!) and that someone from the school had registered a complaint. My daughter and her husband were at work, so I called the lady who ran the senior citizens' program in our neighborhood family resource center down the street. She said not to worry, she'd send over one of the staff members to help.

Coining does leave marks on the body, but I couldn't believe someone would think I was hurting my grandson on purpose. I was so embarrassed. The staff member from the center was able to explain the practice to this lady, and said she would be happy to meet with her supervisor if there were any more questions.

GUIDELINES FOR FAMILY SUPPORT PRACTICE

Key Practice 2: **Create opportunities for families of different backgrounds to identify areas of common ground and to accept and value differences between them.**

Family support programs provide environments in which families can safely explore issues related to parenting and enhance their relationships with their children. When parents of different cultural backgrounds learn that they are facing similar challenges and struggling with similar issues, they enhance their ability to relate to people different from themselves. By identifying common concerns, parents build bridges across their differences with each other. By eliciting and developing respect for different solutions to common challenges, parents may enhance their ability to contribute to their children's positive development and enhance their own ability to flourish in this diverse society.

Some ways for programs to accomplish this are:

● Creating situations in which families have opportunities to meet in ethnically and culturally specific groups and then come together to learn about their differences and to identify concerns that they share.

● Sponsoring programs that bring families of all different backgrounds together around a common concern or experience. For example, one program in San Diego sponsored a panel discussion that included one parent from each of the major ethnic communities it served: Laotian, African American, Anglo, and Latino. Each panelist addressed the questions, "What is your philosophy about how to raise your children?" and "How do you see the school and the school's role?" Hearing the different perspectives allowed families to be more appreciative of each other's situations as well as to recognize their common concerns.

● Developing opportunities for family members in single-ethnic communities to establish meaningful relationships to families from other ethnic backgrounds.

● Offering opportunities for families to acknowledge and utilize each other's strengths and skills. For example, some programs put Spanish-speaking parents and English-speaking parents who want to learn each other's language in touch with each other so that they can exchange lessons.

Guideline D: Programs help families to understand and negotiate the dominant culture and language of the United States.

Key Practice 1: **Serve as a resource for information on how the dominant U.S. culture and institutions function, and how national, state, and local policies affect children and families.**

Family support programs help families to navigate the society of the United States by providing them with information and by helping them develop skills. This is not a new concept; this was one of the functions of early settlement houses. Family support programs often serve as bridges between public institutions and services and families who are unfamiliar with the ways in which these operate. This type of assistance is especially valuable to families who have recently come to this country, those who speak a language other than English at home, and those whose cultural backgrounds are different from that of the mainstream. However, there are families who have been isolated for other reasons, who have recently moved to communities that are very different from those in which they were raised. They too benefit from aspect of family support programs when they encounter certain institutions, agencies, customs, and legal situations for the first time.

Some ways to accomplish this are:

● Providing families with an orientation to the institutions of the United States and to programs with which families are likely to interact—e.g., schools, health and human services agencies, grocery stores, and the police department.

● Offering interested families access to classes in English as a second language and citizenship classes.

● Helping families on a one-on-one basis to resolve difficulties with or to access needed resources from public institutions and agencies.

● Creating parent support groups that enable parents who have been in the United States for varying lengths of time to share their experiences in negotiating the culture in this country and within the local community, and to identify strategies for helping their children become and remain bicultural and bilingual.

● Hiring staff who represent majority and minority ethnic groups and training them to provide information for participants on how the dominant culture works.

● Promoting open communication and dialogue and encouraging people to ask questions. Program staff set an example by showing a willingness to answer and ask well-intentioned questions.

Practice Example

Our families are proud people. They don't like to ask for help—their independence is one of the things that keeps their Palestinian culture alive in their community.

Since there's no Middle Eastern market in our immediate neighborhood, every Wednesday we have "market day": a staff member goes with the women to the supermarket and they all shop together. This may seem like a purely social activity. But many of these women did not have a formal education that included English study, and they have a hard time finding what they need in the store. Also, most of them shopped in open-air markets before they emigrated to the United States, and they're used to being able to see what they're buying. The American style of packaging everything makes shopping difficult for them.

Our program also conducts home visits to give families a chance to ask questions in an environment that they control. I visited Mrs. Arakat when she had just moved to the neighborhood. She was excited about their new apartment and, after a cup of tea, asked me if I'd like to see it. In the kitchen I noticed an unopened case of dog food, so I asked how many dogs they had. She said they didn't have any—and I realized that she must have mistaken the beef-flavored dog food for canned beef. She had resourcefully brought her English-Arabic dictionary to the grocery store, but translating the entire text of each label would have taken forever.

I assured Mrs. Arakat that this type of thing had happened to many, many families—and that we had a special activity on Wednesday mornings for that very reason. We went through the rest of her purchases together and she began the work of learning the English names of her family's favorite foods.

2

Key Practice 2: Teach the skills and strategies parents and staff need in order to work with, participate in, and advocate within institutions and agencies in this society.

Part of helping families negotiate the dominant culture of the United States is helping them understand the power that they have to advocate for themselves and their children. Parents who are new to this country may be completely unfamiliar with its institutions and with how to navigate them; families from socially vulnerable and traditionally disempowered groups often need support, encouragement, skills, information, and allies as they own and exercise their power. Family support programs serve these functions. Family support programs also help parents raised in other countries or cultures to understand that some of the norms of their own cultures may be misunderstood or may not apply here. For example, in many cultures, questioning the judgment of a professional or authority figure is considered disrespectful and wrong. In this country it is perfectly normal and beneficial for parents to attend parent-teacher conferences at their children's school and to discuss their concerns over their children's education with their children's teachers. Not doing so may send the message that the parent does not care.

Some ways to accomplish this are:

- Working with families to identify institutional barriers to their receiving the services they need. Practitioners talk with families about their difficulties accessing services, encouraging them to think about specific ways agencies could make their services more family-friendly for people of their background.

- Helping families learn about their rights and how to access and exercise their power as citizens in a democratic society. Family support workers also partner with families on an individual basis when they are experiencing difficulty in negotiating a particular institution or program.

- Introducing parents to the norms and practices of this society, especially those that conflict with, or differ markedly from, their cultural practices.

- Working with families to understand power relationships within society and to advocate for themselves and their children.

- Sponsoring voter registration drives, spearheading advocacy campaigns, and supporting community organizing activities related to social and economic justice.

Key Practice 3: Work with other agencies and service providers in the community to increase their understanding of and ability to relate to families of different cultural backgrounds.

Communication and cross-cultural understanding are a two-way street. Family support programs are a bridge between families and community institutions, agencies, and service providers. Program staff help families navigate within and negotiate their relationships with mainstream agencies and institutions by working with staff of those institutions to increase their understanding of the families they serve.

Some ways to accomplish this are:

Practice Example

Once you have your antennae up for opportunities to change the system so it works better for families, you start detecting more and more of them. And it seems to me that many of them are totally obvious matters of common sense.

I'm a child protective services worker for the department of social services in a large city in the Southwest. In our city, we have family resource programs attached to every school, as a result of an initiative that began three years ago. About a year ago, the initiative and our department entered into a contract. This resulted in me working approximately ten hours a week as a liaison providing technical assistance to school staff and families on issues of child abuse and neglect.

After working in the schools for two weeks it dawned on me that about half of the families who participate in these programs were Mexican American and spoke Spanish much more fluently than they did English. I also realized that our department had practically no ability to communicate with them. All our telephone receptionists spoke only English, and we didn't have any Spanish-speaking case workers. I raised the issue with my supervisor and kept talking to people about it and trying to get something done. I guess I've become a big advocate. It took some persistence and consciousness-raising, but we now have Spanish telephone lines and two bilingual case workers.

3

E

1

• Developing relationships with other service providers and staff of local agencies. Many programs employ staff on a contract basis who are full-time employees of other public or private family-serving agencies. Most programs encourage their staff members to develop informal contacts within these agencies (see chapter 5).

• Encouraging other providers to take time to learn about the cultures of the families they serve by spending time in the community, asking families about their backgrounds, and reading about the histories of various cultural groups.

• Encouraging other practitioners to question their own assumptions about child rearing, intervention, and other culturally-bound domains.

Practice Example

With the composition of the neighborhood changing, it was probably inevitable that conflicts and tensions would arise at the local family support center. Once largely inhabited by first- and second-generation Italian immigrants, the neighborhood has seen a sizable influx of families from various countries in Central America over the past ten to fifteen years.

Like the neighborhood, the staff of the center is comprised of Salvadorans, Nicaraguans, and Hondurans, and those with an Italian heritage. Conflicts between staff and difficulties in working with some families in the community prompted the center's board to hire a facilitator to conduct an organizational cultural self-assessment.

Maria, a family development specialist, was grateful to be "given permission" to think and talk about these issues. "In my culture—well, at least in my Italian family—we were loud, and we argued even louder. We always interrupted each other, and we often spoke with our hands. My colleague, Rosa, was raised to be much more quiet and calm and not so aggressive. To compound matters, Rosa always viewed our working relationship as a clash in cultures. I just thought it was clash of individual personalities. No wonder we were having trouble communicating!"

"We may still get on each other's nerves from time to time, but at least we'll know why, and we can work on that," says Rosa. "And we're trying harder to respect each other's working styles."

In addition to fostering greater understanding between staff, the self-assessment process prompted the organization to form a work group to develop goals and objectives regarding services for people of different cultures.

• Accompanying parents to appointments. Family support program staff sometimes serve as interpreters and liaisons, helping families and staff of other agencies bridge cultural differences.

Guideline E: Hiring policies and training opportunities reflect the program's priority on affirming diversity.

Key Practice 1: Include staff who reflect the cultural and ethnic experiences and languages of the families with whom they work and integrate their expertise into the entire program.

By representing the cultures of the families served in all staff positions, programs provide the children of families served with role models. This helps to affirm and strengthen their cultural, racial, and linguistic identities.

Some ways for programs to accomplish this are:

• Hiring community residents and instituting training and promotion policies that bring people who reflect the community's composition into leadership.

• Investing time in building staff teams that communicate effectively and work together across differences in culture, race, and language.

• Reviewing program decisions and practices with the entire staff team before implementation.

2

● Involving families in the process of hiring program staff.

Key Practice 2: Provide ongoing staff development on the issues that diversity presents.
Programs support their staff in learning about the issues that diversity presents, so that they can offer participants informal opportunities to learn about and appreciate beliefs and practices that are different from their own. Programs strive to create an environment in which staff can model positive, respectful relationships among people of different ethnic groups and where children see that cultural background does not determine one's place in an organization: leaders come in all cultures, ethnic backgrounds, shapes, sizes, and genders.

Some ways for programs to accomplish this are:

● Hiring staff from different cultural, ethnic, and linguistic backgrounds. Programs serving predominately single-ethnic populations may want to have most of their staff represent that group.

● Linking with a family support program in another neighborhood or with a different ethnic, cultural, racial, and linguistic make-up. Programs may sponsor joint activities or forums.

● Conducting an organization-wide cultural self assessment. Many programs undertake this process with the help of a trained facilitator.

● Providing staff with information about how culture contributes to the development of children's identity.

● Creating opportunities for staff to reflect on how race, language, and culture have impacted their own development and beliefs as well as their way of interacting with families. Programs provide staff development sessions that encourage staff to develop cultural competence. Programs enable staff to attend workshops and conferences that will help them work effectively in different ethnic and cultural communities. Programs also give staff access to workshops, retreats, and other methods of staff development on working respectfully in multiethnic situations and ethnically diverse communities.

● Encouraging ongoing communication among staff and families. Programs provide staff with skills in helping families find common ground. Program staff and administrators encourage all who come in contact with the program to see differences as differences and not as deficits.

● Encouraging staff to raise concerns with each other about incidents or interpersonal dynamics that they find troubling.

Affirming Diversity: Challenges in Practice

1. Learning about other cultures and ethnic groups can sometimes lead to creating or reinforcing stereotypes.

Programs use a variety of strategies to create a welcoming, affirming atmosphere in their programs, consistent with the ethnic or cultural backgrounds of the families they serve. Decorations and holiday events have an important role to play in sending messages that the traditions of the culture are valued. But these outward expressions of cultural identity can ring hollow without attention to the underlying meanings they represent and genuine ownership by the families who participate in the program. For example, draping walls in kinte cloth and lighting Kwaanza candles does not necessarily show respect for African American families, particularly if families in the program have other strong traditions that are more important to them than Kwaanza or if they have little knowledge of or interest in Kwaanza. Having parents take the lead in planning special cultural events and other ways that the program expresses support for cultural identity is critical to ensuring a match between the program's intent to be respectful and the participants' own cultural identities.

2. Creating an atmosphere of affirmation for each family's cultural identity can be difficult in a program with many different cultures represented among its participants.

A number of family support programs face the challenge of serving families of many different ethnic and cultural groups, each speaking a different language or dialect. Even the minimal requirement of being able to communicate with each family may be difficult to meet within the staffing limitations of the program. This extreme diversity of participants underscores the necessity for affirming each group in an appropriate way and finding ways for diverse groups to understand one another. The program can use a seeming disadvantage to its advantage by working to create an atmosphere of openness that includes all the cultural groups it serves.

Programs have discovered that they can work creatively with the families in the program and with community residents outside the program to create necessary avenues for communication and understanding. The need for translation can offer opportunities for developing strong bonds among families of the same linguistic background. An atmosphere of learning in the program can encourage families to teach others about their values and beliefs, and to be open to what they learn from others.

3. Helping families negotiate aspects of the dominant culture they need for survival while affirming their own cultural identity requires a careful balance.

Families who are not of the dominant culture sometimes need tools and information to advocate for themselves in the context of the dominant culture. Family support programs have a responsibility to see that families understand how to get the resources they need for themselves and their children. Responding to legal requirements, filling out applications, participating in interviews, or asking for assistance from human service systems can be a daunting experience for a family unaccustomed to the culture or language in which these systems operate. In these cases, family support staff can be useful interpreters of language and custom for families who need to navigate these systems. Staff can help families understand what their rights are, what the system is asking of them, and how to access it most easily.

At the same time, programs also share responsibility for helping families affirm their own ways. Families should not feel that they are required to give up their beliefs and values or make themselves "more presentable" in order to get necessary resources for their families. Staff can be helpful in pointing out the differences in cultural expectations and the choices that families can make in dealing with the dominant culture when it presents a conflict. For example, a health examination may include asking patients to reveal aspects of their sexual life that are off-limits for discussion in their culture, particularly in the company of men and women together. Family support staff can brief the family on what to expect ahead of time and make sure that they understand that they can request a private conference or another alternative to the usual interview. Staff also have the responsibility to approach the medical provider to request changes in protocols that would be more respectful of the family's culture.

4. Creating a program atmosphere where staff and families feel comfortable discussing and sharing perspectives about issues of race, language, and culture can be difficult.

The program's overall atmosphere of acceptance and willingness to hear and reflect the voices of all its participants is key to an environment where differences can be explored and affirmed. This atmosphere is developed in many different ways from program policies to staff practices. Governance structure, staffing patterns, and other administrative aspects of the program are as important as the interaction among staff and between staff and family participants in sending messages about the relative importance of different cultural groups. Inclusion in decision making at all levels is a critical measure of how the program views the different groups that make up its population.

Interactions among staff and families establish the "culture of the program," define the level of trust and determine the extent to which people can feel comfortable revealing potential disagreements and working to resolve them. Training for staff, ongoing discussion, and safe, intentional mechanisms for airing differences and encouraging exploration are all important elements of a long-term commitment to diversity.

Principle Five
Programs are embedded in their communities and contribute to the community-building process.

Principle Six
Programs advocate with families for services and systems that are fair, responsive, and accountable to the families served.

Principle Seven
Practitioners work with families to mobilize formal and informal resources to support family development.

Family support programs have always acknowledged the impact of the community on the families who live there and on the development of their children. Programs in recent years have expanded beyond the role of service providers and have actively worked to promote the health and well-being of their neighborhoods and communities. They have also begun to take a leadership role in identifying and advocating for changes that need to be made in public service systems to make them more responsive to the needs of families. This chapter examines the responsibility of programs to take an active role in their communities, and discusses the ways in which programs carry out this responsibility.

Some scholars believe that the community is the parent to the family.[1] Families are significantly affected by the support, resources, and opportunities that are available to them in their communities, just as children are affected by their families. Many factors that influence a family's capacity to nurture children lie outside of the family itself, in the neighborhood in which the family lives, and in the array of resources to which the family has access.[2]

Institutionalized racism, inadequate housing, and economic deprivation often affect whole communities and significantly diminish the ability of families to promote the optimal development of their children.[3] The cumulative effect of these sources of stress on an individual family or on a whole community cannot be adequately addressed by any one family support program or service provider, no matter how good it is. A comprehensive array of coordinated programs, services, and resources is required to ameliorate the immediate negative impact on families of these deeply rooted problems, to

address their causes, and to press for long-term solutions.[4]

While earlier intervention models focused on working with individual families, family support programs reflect a broader outlook: one that sees community building as key to supporting family life. Family resource centers often serve not only as places at which families can meet their own needs, but as points of "congregation where community-building occurs ... they create the 'social capital' needed for communities to experience growth."[5] Developing social capital that reinforces family development is a responsibility that neighborhood initiatives to improve children's and families' outcomes cannot afford to overlook.

What Is Community?

Community, in the context of family support practice, has several different meanings. First, it identifies the geographic location of a program and the area in which families participating in the program reside. In this sense, the community may consist of a number of city blocks that make up a neighborhood, a school attendance area, a whole township, or a thinly populated rural area that covers many square miles. Second, community refers to a group of people who share an affiliation, such as a culture, religion, or other set of beliefs, values, or interests. This kind of community can include, for example, parents whose children attend the same school, families who live in the same public housing development, or people who speak the same language. Third, community can refer to a group of people who support each other for the good of the whole group. These different meanings of community can be applied simultaneously, and families belong to more than one kind of community at a time. This chapter concentrates on the first type of community, the residential community, which is strongly shaped by the other affiliations and groups that exist within it.

How Programs Build Community

Family support programs promise to be full partners with families and the communities in which they live. Keeping this promise means going beyond the boundaries of the program itself, and taking into consideration the whole environment in which families live and grow. The goal is to create a program that is shaped by the concerns, desires, and values of community members. Programs that are embedded in the community help families develop connections to others who give and receive support, thereby benefitting families' long-term development.

When communities have "ownership" of programs, programs endure and enable families to achieve results over the long-term.[6] A test of the program's integration into the community is the extent to which community residents feel invested in the program, know who is in control, and are confident that their values are shared by the program. The challenge for programs that are initiated from outside of the community is to view their leadership as transitional and make every effort to become owned by—and not just based in—the community. [7]

Programs that are successfully embedded in their communities usually have several common characteristics. They collaborate with other providers of resources and support in the community. They work with parents to plan and carry out services and activities. They serve as catalysts to community-wide growth and progress. And they create a sense of community among participants.

Family support programs and services almost always work in concert with other local service providers to make sure that all families are able to access the resources they need. Program administrators and staff collaborate with other service providers to assess the community's needs and resources and to plan services and programs accordingly. This includes identifying changes that would result in more effective services for families and advocating for those services, whether they would directly affect families participating in the program or not.

Programs also collaborate with parent participants in developing services (see chapter 3), thereby underscoring their total commitment to sharing power with parents at every level. As they interact with others in the community, family support programs model a real partnership with parents and create opportunities for parents to speak for themselves outside of the program.

Family support programs strive to be catalysts for the well-being of the communities around them. Family support programs cannot offer all things to all families; their success depends on their ability to increase families' opportunities to grow and obtain support from others in their community. Programs view themselves as permanent parts of their communities and they maintain a long-term commitment to strengthening every potential resource for families.

In addition to serving as a catalyst in the overall community, programs work to create a sense of community within the program. Staff work to create a network of families who help each other, learn from each other, and work together to address issues of common concern. By assisting families in attaining skills, information, and opportunities to socialize and work together, programs build microcosms of a healthy community. Families can build on the self-confidence and skills they have acquired within the program to advocate more effectively for what they need outside of the program. (See chapter 3 for more on this topic.)

Advocating with Families for Services and Systems that Are Fair, Responsive, and Accountable

As leaders in their communities, family support programs are responsible for articulating a vision of services that are inclusive, equitable, just, responsive, and accountable to families. Family support programs strive to be more than providers of preventive or remedial services. Their aim is to promote the well-being of children and families in every possible way. Parents depend on schools, healthcare and childcare providers, and other public and private sources of support to help them give their children full opportunities for growth and development. Parents have a vested interest in the quality of these systems and a right to hold them accountable for providing what their children need.

Family support programs have a responsibility to support parents in claiming that right, and they uphold that responsibility in a number of ways. They assist families in attaining the skills and knowledge necessary to participate in making decisions about the services and resources they need.

Programs also join forces with families to strengthen their capacity to serve as mediators and advocates for their own members in getting these services and resources.[8] They assist families in becoming their own "case managers" and assist parents in becoming effective advocates for their children in school and in other arenas. Family support staff know that whereas their programs facilitate families' self-determination while they are participating in the program, families operate primarily in the world outside of the program. Parents' capacity to exert control over this environment is critical to their progress and to their children's development.[9]

Many families are marginalized from mainstream society by poverty, racism, and linguistic differences or other distinctions. Disproportionate numbers of these families depend on public systems for resources they need, and thus have a greater stake than others in the accessibility of those systems. At the same time, these marginalized families often have less power within these systems to change them, fewer advocates for their concerns, and less of the information and other resources that would allow them to advocate for themselves. Community-based programs can play a catalytic role in enabling these families in particular to exert their own power and get what they need.[10]

Helping families to empower themselves to change community conditions and influence the allocation of resources is essential to long-term community building. Programs play a critical role in helping families be more effective, empowered participants in decisions that affect their communities. Programs by themselves cannot change many of the conditions that affect families. When families are informed about community-wide issues and act on that information, over time they can have an impact on the health of their communities and the resources available to them. As community members experience greater control over services and institutions, their feelings of ownership and commitment to those services and institutions—and their likelihood of working to improve them—increase.

As more control over resources is placed in the hands of states and communities, family support programs increasingly are expected to play a role in community-wide planning and collaboration with public agencies. Because services are best planned by those closest to their recipients, publicly funded family support initiatives are often charged with planning and integrating services on a community-wide basis.[11] The Federal Family Preservation and Support Services Program, passed in 1993, initiated broad-based planning in every state to encourage more state- and community-level collaboration among all programs serving children and families.[12]

The movement toward collaborative, community-based efforts is likely to continue—and to require local programs to understand and collaborate with public service systems while maintaining their independence and their non-categorical approach to families. While it is important for programs to work with public service agencies, it is also vital that they remain oriented toward advocating for change in those agencies. Community-based programs that have been developed as part of state or local initiatives which are based on a family support approach are specifically intended to produce changes in the systems of which they are a part.

The Importance of Formal and Informal Resources

Formal community resources that are available to families include the institutions and services that are administered by public agencies (such as schools, parks, housing assistance, and substance abuse treatment) or by individual professionals (such as doctors and school social workers) as well as community institutions (such as religious groups and youth clubs). Most families can utilize these basic services provided they know where they are and have the resources needed to get them.

Informal resources are the many types of resources that friends, neighbors, co-workers, and relatives provide to families in the course of daily life, which include loving care, information, advice, and material assistance. This network is almost always the first place to which families turn when they are having problems.[13] The definition of a family's social network and the kinds of support it provides may vary greatly from one family to the next. The family's cultural background is particularly important in defining both of these things. Regardless of these differences, though, the networks that provide informal resources are based on reciprocity that community members build over time as they assist one another in a variety of ways in response to their changing needs.

While high-quality formal services are vital to families when they need them, informal resources are equally important.[14] Communities depend on their informal networks of resources to support individual members and to create a shared sense of community. Family support programs work to foster "interdependencies among community members in ways that promote the flow of resources to (and from) families."[15]

NOTES

[1] Garbarino, J. (1982) *Children and families in the social environment.* (New York: Aldine Publishing).

[2] Hobbs, N., P. R. Dokecki, K. V. Hoover-Dempsey, R.M. Moroney, M.W. Shayne, and K.H. Weeks (1984) *Strengthening families.* (San Francisco, Calif.: Jossey-Bass).

[3] Pinderhughes, E. (1989) *Understanding race, ethnicity, and power: The key to efficacy in clinical practice.* (New York: Free Press).

[4] Canada, G. (1993) "Nothing but trouble." *City Limits Magazine.* (New York: City Limits).

[5] Bruner, C. (1996) "Realizing a vision for children, families and neighborhoods: An alternative to other modest proposals." Paper presented at the Carter Center National Leadership Forum on Community Strategies for Children and Families, February 14–16.

"Social capital" is defined as "a largely nonprofessional, voluntary, rich and layered network of social activities and behaviors within a community that afford children, families, and youth the opportunity to congregate, share experiences and interests, and realize some of their aspirations in a way that enhances overall community cohesion. [Bruner, C. (1995) "Towards defining government's role as a catalyst: Building social capital in disinvested communities." Occasional Paper Number 16. (Des Moines, Iowa: Child and Family Policy Center) 3.]

[6] Farrow, F. (1994) "Family support on the federal policy agenda." In S. L. Kagan and B. Weissbourd, eds., *Putting families first: America's family support movement and the challenge of change.* (San Francisco, Calif.: Jossey-Bass) 363.

[7] Reissman, F. and D. Carroll (1995) *Redefining self-help: Policy and practice.* (San Francisco, Calif.: Jossey-Bass).

[8] Kagan, S. L. and A. Shelley (1987) "The promise and problems of family support programs." In S. L. Kagan, D.R. Powell, B. Weissbourd, and E. Zigler, eds., *America's family support programs: The origins and development of a movement.* (New Haven, Conn.: Yale University Press) 9–10.

[9] Basch, M. (1975) "Toward a theory that encompasses depression: A revision of existing causal hypotheses in psychoanalysis." In J. Anthony and T. Benedek, eds., *Depression and human existence.* (Boston, Mass.: Brown) 513.

GUIDELINES FOR FAMILY SUPPORT PRACTICE

[10] Pinderhughes, E., (1989) *Understanding race, ethnicity, and power: The key to efficacy in clinical practice.* (New York: Free Press) 109–146.

[11] Massinga, R. (1994) "Transforming social services: Family supportive strategies." In S. L. Kagan and B. Weissbourd, eds., *Putting families first: America's family support movement and the challenge of change.* (San Francisco, Calif.: Jossey-Bass) 97.

[12] United States Department of Health and Human Services (1994) Program instructions for family preservation and support service programs, Title IVB of the Child Welfare and Adoption Assistance Act, H.R. 2264, Omnibus Budget Reconciliation Act of 1993.

[13] Cochran, M. "Personal social networks as a focus of support." In D. O. Unger and D. R. Powell, eds., *Families as nurturing systems: Support across the lifespan.* (Binghampton, N.Y.: The Haworth Press) 45–67.

Norton, D. G., J. Morales, and E. Andrews (1980) "The neighborhood self-help project." Occasional Paper Number 9. (Chicago, Ill.: School of Social Services Administration, University of Chicago).

[14] Dunst, C., C. Trivette, and A. Deal (1988) *Enabling and empowering families: Principles and guidelines for practice.* (Cambridge, Mass:, Brookline Books) 23–34.

[15] Dunst, C. and C. Trivette (1994) "Aims and principles of family support programs." In Dunst, C., C. Trivette, and A. Deal, eds., *Supporting and strengthening families, Vol. 1: Methods, strategies, and practices.* (Cambridge, Mass.: Brookline Books) 37.

Programs in Communities: Guidelines for Practice

Family support programs are actively engaged in building the communities in which they are located. This community-building process is multi-faceted: it enhances residents' sense of belonging to a community and being related to each another; builds the community's infrastructure and works with others to change systems and policies to make them increasingly supportive of families; and increases and improves the connections between and among people and institutions in the community. Programs engage in community building because they understand that healthy communities nurture families and provide environments in which children grow and prosper.

Guidelines and Key Practices

Guideline A: Programs facilitate a sense of belonging and a connection to the community among program participants.

Key Practices
1. Emphasize the positive aspects and achievements of the community and encourage participants' sense of responsibility for the community's well-being.
2. Encourage participants to take part in community activities and to avail themselves of community resources.
3. Be a resource for and promote positive relations among different cultural, ethnic, and socioeconomic groups in the community.
4. Ensure that the program's location is easily accessible for families.

Guideline B: Programs identify and develop networks of support in the community that are available to participants.

Key Practices
1. Identify informal support systems that exist in the community and put families in touch with them.
2. Work with families to effectively use formal systems of support.

Guideline C: Programs respond to community issues and engage families as partners in this process.

Key Practices
1. Develop an understanding of community issues and use this understanding to guide all of the program's work with families.
2. Develop specific programmatic responses to community-identified needs and priorities.
3. Prepare parents to be advocates and leaders on community issues and support them in these roles.
4. Promote awareness of and joint responses to community issues among the general public and among other community agencies and institutions.

Guideline D: Programs work to develop a coordinated response to community needs.

Key Practices
1. Participate in community-wide planning efforts.
2. Collaborate with other community institutions and agencies in tangible ways.
3. Promote accountability in human services delivery systems that ensures effective services for families.
4. Work to secure adequate resources to support the healthy development of children and families in the community.
5. Help families to make their voices heard as they advocate for change.

Guideline A: Programs facilitate a sense of belonging and a connection to the community among program participants.

Key Practice 1: Emphasize the positive aspects and achievements of the community and encourage participants' sense of responsibility for the community's well-being.

Focusing on the strengths and achievements of the community fosters community pride. When residents, especially youth and young adults, feel good about the place in which they live and the others who live there, it helps them to feel good about themselves. When residents are proud of their community, they are likely to feel invested in its long-term success. They are more likely to work to improve the community and to continue to live there and raise a family there. Residents can make a very real difference in the community: When residents feels ownership of their community and act on its behalf, they work to make the neighborhood a safer and healthier place to live and work.

Some ways for programs to accomplish this are:

● Organizing community improvement activities. Examples of these include garbage clean-up campaigns, mural painting, community service initiatives for youth, anti-drug marches, and renovation projects.

● Researching the history of the community and sharing information about its achievements. Program staff seek to uncover strengths of the community and to provide families with information about its history. Programs share this information through events (such as a "history night"), their newsletters, articles in community newspapers, a "community corner" located at the program's site, and through conversations between program staff and participants.

● Providing opportunities for participants to identify with the center and the community. For example, some programs make and sell T-shirts; others sponsor floats in holiday parades.

Practice Example

A vacant lot, overgrown with weeds, near a family resource center had become a dumping ground for all sorts of garbage, including broken beer bottles and the used needles of drug addicts who went there at night to get high. The eyesore had lowered neighborhood morale and discouraged participation at the program. Parents were afraid to walk past it with their children—especially after dark—and so would not attend activities.

The center's parent advisory committee and staff organized a spring clean-up weekend in early May. The parents took responsibility for recruiting workers and volunteers to supply cold drinks and food for them. The staff rounded up the necessary equipment: shovels, wheel barrows, work gloves, and a large city dumpster in which to throw all the garbage. More than two dozen families volunteered to work for at least part of the weekend. Even the youngest children were pressed into service as water boys and girls, bringing the thirsty workers beverages.

Following this major community project, the parents involved in the clean-up began a neighborhood watch program and talked to the local police department about patrolling the area more frequently. The center staff and parents organized "touch-up" days periodically to maintain the safety and cleanliness of the lot. But they never had much to clean up. Since the neighborhood had reclaimed the lot, the drug addicts and others who misused the plot moved on.

Key Practice 2: Encourage participants to take part in community activities and to avail themselves of community resources.

When families participate in activities and utilize resources that the community offers—whether formal or informal, ongoing or one-time—they feel more connected to their community. Families who become involved can help shape community activities and events, and their input results in programs that reflect their preferences and values. By participating in community activities and using community resources, families demonstrate that those activities and resources are important to them and help ensure that they will be available in the future.

Some ways for programs to accomplish this are:

● Using a variety of means to let program participants know about community activities. Programs post information about community events on bulletin boards and publicize them in newsletters. Some programs designate a space as the "community corner" and put community-related information such as flyers, newspapers, referral lists, descriptions of job openings, participants' tips on local resources, restaurants, and services, etc.

● Being involved in planning community activities. Programs may cosponsor activities with other community agencies or institutions. Program staff and parents may participate in planning committees.

● Building awareness of community activities and resources into the development of program components. Many programs offer information and referral services. Staff of these programs tell family members about other community agencies and institutions that could be resources to them. Some programs schedule events or components that complement specific community activities.

● Facilitating families' participation in community events. Programs may provide transportation or childcare during events or hold activities at the center that are sponsored by other entities. Some programs encourage participants and staff to attend community events and activities together as a group.

Practice Example

Our center, along with the businesses on the street, co-sponsors a community arts festival every summer where everyone enjoys live music, food from local restaurants, and crafts. Local artists, including teenagers and youth, display and sell their work. Our participating families staff a food booth and the information booth. We also coordinate the musical performances. Proceeds from food sales are used to fund other activities at the center throughout the year. Our families have lot of fun and take pride in being the hosts of the festival. It helps promote teamwork and camaraderie.

The community in which our center is located is diverse. Residents include middle-income African American families, newly arrived Haitian immigrants, some "yuppies" who have recently started moving into the loft conversion buildings a few blocks away, and professors and students from the nearby university. They all come to the festival! We've earned a reputation for having the hottest music and best food in town. I guess there's nothing like a great party to bring people together and promote good will.

3

Key Practice 3: Be a resource for and promote positive relations among different cultural, ethnic, and socioeconomic groups in the community.

An important goal of community building is to improve communication and relationships between different groups in the community so that they can work together for the betterment of the whole. Programs strive to be inclusive and to model a cohesive community that respects and honors diversity. This holds equally true when a program's participants are reflective of the larger community as when the program is targeted to a specific subgroup within that community. By welcoming all families, by being a place at which communication can occur, and by honoring differences while emphasizing common goals, programs help families feel more connected to each other, more supported by each other, and less alienated and alone.

Some ways for programs to accomplish this are:

- Providing services and activities that promote interaction and communication among people of different cultural, ethnic, and socioeconomic backgrounds. For example, programs host open houses and other events that are open to all community members, organize ethnic events, produce materials in the languages spoken by potential program participants, and provide translators. Programs may offer forums and workshops for teenagers on race relations, or incorporate discussions of the differences in child-rearing practices among cultures as part of parent education classes, or plan and sponsor a community activity in which all community members are equally invested.

- Conducting outreach to assure participation by different community groups. Programs that seek to serve groups that traditionally have been separate from each other, sometimes must conduct creative outreach efforts to maximize participation and break down barriers. For example, programs have outreach staff that reflect the composition of the community, and they organize multi-ethnic or multi-group events such as potlucks, U.N. Nights, and multi-generational events.

- Using a variety of formal and informal means to publicize the program among residents. Programs use a variety of outreach methods, including articles in local newspapers, public service announcements on radio and television, flyers, and canvassing. Many programs encourage staff members to interact informally with residents in a variety of ways, such as helping with a parent patrol in school or park areas. Word of mouth is a most effective way of creating interest in the program. Families who have benefited from the program will "talk it up" among their friends and neighbors.

- Ensuring that the program's service menu reflects the interests of each ethnic group in the community.

- Lending program resources to community residents. Some programs allow groups of residents to use their photocopy and fax machines. Others provide transportation, childcare, staff expertise, and space in the program's newsletter. Many programs provide space for community residents to come together to discuss and otherwise address mutual concerns.

- Publicizing the program's advocacy efforts on behalf of all children and families in the community. For example, if the program is advocating for safer streets, staff might post notices inviting adults and youth from the community to take part in a town meeting or a letter-writing campaign urging the city to install street lamps.

- Staffing the program with people whose backgrounds represent the diversity of the community. Relations among staff members may serve as a model for families of diverse backgrounds communicating and relating to each other positively.

Key Practice 4: Ensure that the program's location is easily accessible for families.

One of the ways in which community-based programs communicate their role in the community is by their location. By being geographically central and occupying a location that is convenient and free of negative associations to families, programs identify themselves positively in the community and increase the likelihood that residents will participate.

4

B

1

Practice Example

As a staff member of a substance abuse prevention and counseling program, I was frustrated. We had hardly any contact with teachers or mental health care providers. How could we help people recover from drug dependency and accomplish their goals without knowing more about their work with others who were trying to do the same? How could we educate teens and children without being in touch with teachers? Things were really spread out in our rural community, which made things even worse. People had a hard time getting to school, let alone to three or four different service providers.

Two other counselors, our boss, and I called a meeting. We invited families who had used our services, plus other family-serving organizations, agencies, and individuals. They invited the people they serve. After a series of open discussions, the community decided they needed a centrally located, attractive place that would show how much the community valued its children, teens, parents, grandparents, and on up! It needed to coordinate a wide variety of services and make them easy to get to.

Parents knew we'd need lots of time to secure funding, and they wanted to get the whole community involved, so they made a plan to spread the word and raise money. They made a list of possible fundraisers and they've made their way through almost all: bowling tournaments, raffles—you name it. Some helped write proposals and gave testimonials to get funding from federal, state, local, foundation, and corporate sources.

It's been an intense five years. Our center still smells like new paint; it's brimming with activity. We're kind of in the center of town, easy to get to. In addition to coming here for services and programs—the county health department, a family service agency, WIC, and our program are some of the agencies that are co-located here—the community uses the center for everything from bingo to PTA meetings. It's hard to remember the days when talking to a participant's social worker meant a long-distance phone call. Now there are some right down the hall!

Some ways for programs to accomplish this are:

- Choosing a location carefully. Program planners investigate community demographics and dynamics before selecting a site that is freestanding or shared with another agency, in order to choose a location that won't alienate groups of families. For example, in communities in which there are gangs, a community-based program would be located on neutral turf. If many parents in the program's target population have had negative experiences in school, planners would take this into consideration before sharing facilities with the local elementary school.

- Going to where the parents are. Programs are often located in places to which parents go regularly, such as schools, childcare centers, workplaces, shopping malls, and waiting rooms of medical clinics. Home visiting programs connect with families in their homes.

- Facilitating families' travel to the program. Some programs provide transportation. Others make sure to locate themselves near public transportation or parking lots, depending on the modes of transportation that families in the community use.

- Providing means of access for families who have special physical needs (such as ramps and lifts for wheelchairs).

Guideline B: Programs identify and develop networks of support in the community that are available to participants.

Key Practice 1: Identify informal support systems that exist in the community and put families in touch with them.

Informal associations are a primary source of support and resources for families. Informal support systems arise out of common interests, and generally do not stigmatize or label people. Informal support comes from neighbors, friends, and families, and can extend to such groups as parents and other caregivers who bring children to the same park regularly, dog-walkers who frequent a certain park in the morning, and a neighborhood woman who gives piano lessons in her home for free. Informal support also comes from organized groups such as neighborhood associations and block clubs; bowling, softball, and other athletic leagues; and local chapters of organizations such as the Parent Teacher Association, 4H, and Rotary

Club. (For more information on helping families to identify sources of informal support networks, see chapter 3, guideline A, key practice 3.)

Some ways for programs to accomplish this are:

● Conducting a community assessment of informal resources and natural leaders. To uncover informal resources, program staff talk extensively to participants. Some programs canvass neighborhoods door-to-door to survey residents on resources with which they are familiar. In the course of talking to community residents, names of natural leaders usually emerge. These natural leaders are people in the community to whom others look for support and help, such as a woman who provides milk and cookies to neighborhood children after school or a man who fixes cars and enjoys talking to people.

● Providing space, materials, or supplies to informal groups.

● Building on personal relationships. Program staff use their personal contacts and the contacts of participants to connect families with people who can provide the resources that they need. Staff and other parents make introductions when appropriate.

● Identifying and regularly communicating with official and natural community leaders. Community leaders can provide insight and information about community resources. Programs encourage linkage and communication among leaders, the program, and families in the community.

Practice Example

Due to complications at birth, my daughter, Alicia, was born mildly developmentally disabled, and with physical disabilities that somewhat limit her mobility. Our state has a special program for families with children with disabilities, and we've been involved in the program for a number of years. They've helped us gain access to the special educational and therapy programs that Alicia has needed.

But just as important as putting us in touch with services and professionals has been the emotional support they've given us. They organize activities that allow us to meet other families who have children with special needs. We've met some of our best friends this way.

They also arrange opportunities for Alicia to get out and just be a kid—doing what most kids like to do. For example, they helped Alicia into a local junior bowling league. First they worked with her until she'd learned the game and then they provided her with transportation each Saturday morning to and from the bowling lanes. Bowling has been a great confidence builder. Her physical limitations aren't a big factor in this sport, and she's made friends. One time, the van that the program uses broke down and she didn't make it to bowling. The other kids on the league and their parents were so upset by her absence that they promised to pick her up and drop her off in the future—and they have!

Key Practice 2: Work with families to effectively use formal systems of support.

Families may need and be eligible for resources available through the human services delivery system. Large, complicated systems such as our public human services system can be formidable, intimidating, and difficult to navigate for the uninitiated. Practitioners inform families about support from both public and private sources and help them access this support.

Some ways to accomplish this are:

● Sharing information. Practitioners inform families about the laws and rights that govern access to information (such as laws guaranteeing freedom of information, consumer protection laws, and laws that protect confidentiality and limit access to personal records). They also provide information about the structures and procedures of school systems, health care systems, child welfare systems, immigration agencies, financial institutions and social services systems.

● Helping families develop the skills they need to access formal resources. Practitioners model assertiveness, effective communication, and self-advocacy. They also use role-playing to help

2

families develop their own skills and confidence. Many programs link families who need resources available through formal systems with families who have experience navigating the system or to allies within those systems.

● Helping families access the resources they need. Practitioners frequently accompany families when they seek information and resources, and provide translation services when necessary. Practitioners develop relationships with service professionals in the system and rely on these contacts to improve families' experiences.

Guideline C: Programs respond to community issues and engage families as partners in this process.

Key Practice 1: Develop an understanding of community issues and use this understanding to guide all of the program's work with families.

In order for a program to maintain credibility and legitimacy in the eyes of families, program staff must know what's going on in the community through the eyes of families. Practitioners and programs remain responsive to residents and effective in part by understanding the issues that families in the community confront daily. Programs strive to infuse recognition of community issues into all facets of program operations and to build in feedback loops to keep their information current.

Some ways for programs to accomplish this are:

● Conducting an assessment of community needs and resources. Formal community assessment that focuses on strengths and resources as well as problems and needs, and which involves community residents in the process, is invaluable. Program staff review existing assessments and solicit feedback from community members in a variety of ways, including surveys, interviews, focus groups, public meetings and meetings of service providers. Community assessment should be ongoing, and information should be updated periodically so that the program can continue to respond to the community's concerns and priorities, even as they change.

● Listening to program participants. Program staff use consumer satisfaction surveys, feedback from participants, suggestion boxes, and other information-gathering mechanisms to inform formal evaluations and to track the extent to which families think the program is responding to community needs.

● Learning from others in the community. Program staff participate in community forums; attend school board meetings; read local newspapers; and pay attention to talks and reports given by others, such as local lawmakers and school board members.

● Providing continual training for staff. Programs provide time and opportunities for staff to discuss community issues, and make a point of creating an atmosphere of learning. Many programs provide opportunities for staff to learn from parents such as parent presentations in staff meetings.

Key Practice 2: Develop specific programmatic responses to community-identified needs and priorities.

Understanding community-identified needs and priorities is central to creating a program that serves the community and that community members trust. Programs that fail to respond to input lose credibility and alienate potential participants. Programs should commit resources to being responsive to changing community priorities, developing creative ways to respond when funding is limited.

Some ways for programs to accomplish this are:

● Establishing working groups and coalitions. Many programs are able to gain more resources to address community needs by working in partnership with families, agencies, institutions, government, the business community, churches, and other groups.

● Pursuing additional funding or reallocating current resources to respond to emerging issues. Programs look for Requests for Proposals (RFPs) that address the needs of families in the community.

● Structuring program components to satisfy community needs. Programs offer activities, classes, and workshops that address needs that the community has expressed. Some programs also provide jobs for community members, and spend money in the community in a variety of ways. Community needs are incorporated into plans for expansion or development.

● Being there for communities when there is a crisis. For example, if a community suffers a natural disaster like a hurricane, an earthquake, or a fire, by remaining open, persevering under difficult conditions, and mobilizing help for residents in need, a family support program demonstrates its commitment to the community and to the children and families who live there.

Key Practice 3: Prepare parents to be advocates and leaders on community issues and support them in these roles.

Parents can be their own best advocates and the most effective spokespersons for their needs. Not only do residents draw the most persuasive picture of their community they also have the most to gain by advocating for the community. By speaking for themselves and their families, par-

Practice Example

I'd never say I'm glad the big hurricane happened. It took the lives of people I loved. It cost the city and all of us millions of dollars. But something good did come of it: it made us a community.

Recent immigrants from Belize, Nicaragua, and the Dominican Republic and relatively well-established Anglo, Haitian, and Cuban families live in our neighborhood; and there have been tensions. In the past few years expensive condos began to be built in the predominately poor neighborhood where new and younger immigrants live, and wealthier Cuban and Anglo families began moving in. The tensions were mounting.

Nature doesn't discriminate. The storm ruined property and claimed lives in all groups. In its aftermath, the family resource center, located in the elementary school, stayed open when everything else (even the school) had shut down. The center's director, Yolanda, kept it open. It was whatever families needed it to be: a place to sleep, a collection and dissemination point for emergency supplies, even a church! Both of our area's Catholic churches, one far wealthier than the other, were nearly destroyed. Yolanda knew staff in the religious education programs of both parishes, and asked them if their priests would want to use the center to hold a shared mass. It was a beautiful service, and it brought the communities together to get to know each other. Families had a potluck lunch together afterward at the center.

Everyone really believes in the center now. Before the hurricane it had focused on helping families when their children had trouble in school. Afterwards, Yolanda saw that the need for emergency clothing, food, and shelter didn't end when the damage was fixed. The center has kept on providing those services. Parents of all ethnic groups and local businesses and churches have gotten involved to make them possible. Yolanda also started creating forums for us parents to talk openly about our differences and for our kids to work together on joint projects. I'm sorry it took such a crisis, but I'm glad we became a community.

PROGRAMS IN COMMUNITIES

ents build relationships with other residents and institutions that enable them to more effectively protect and nurture their children. Staff join with parents to facilitate their advocacy efforts, develop concrete strategies for improving practices and policies, and assure that services and policies are more accountable to the people whom they are intended to serve.

Practice Example

When my husband left me and the kids, I don't know how we would have survived without the family support program and its childcare program. The center's staff gave me lots of emotional help after the divorce. And without the childcare subsidies, I never would have been able to pay for day care out of my salary. I probably would have had to go on welfare. All of the other parents in the program feel the same way. We often think about the many other parents we know who are in the same boat but who are on a waiting list for childcare help.

Yet each year, some state legislator thinks it's a good idea to cut the state's childcare budget. The staff at our program has helped us to understand how the budget process could affect our own subsidies and the people who are on the waiting lists. Our program is part of a statewide coalition that keeps track of things in the state capitol.

When a proposal that could be dangerous is up for consideration, the center writes up a fact sheet for us parents that includes suggestions of things we can do about it. Sometimes, if time is short, they let us use the center's telephone to call our representatives long-distance when we stop by to drop off or pick up our children. They organize parents' meetings so that we can plan for what we want to do. Last spring, we decided we wanted to go to the capitol ourselves. The center staff chartered a bus and helped us practice what we would say in meetings with the lawmakers.

The representative of the district where the center is located is very supportive. The center helps us organize little ways of saying thank you. Each June our kids make homemade Father's Day cards to send to him, and we always invite him to the special activities we plan. Some of the staff and parents volunteer in his re-election campaign in their free time, handing out flyers and stuffing envelopes.

Some ways for programs to accomplish this are:

● Helping parents understand how their personal situations relate to public policies. Programs provide timely information on local, state, and federal issues, how they will affect families in the community, and ways families can respond to them. Many programs keep families informed by distributing fact sheets, newsletters, and action alerts that other organizations have produced and by forming telephone chains. Program staff keep abreast of developments that could affect residents by adding their names to mailing lists of watchdog organizations, keeping in touch with or joining national organizations, and subscribing to an on-line computer service that specialize in family issues.

● Providing leadership training. Programs provide parents opportunities to develop leadership skills through forums, workshops, and courses offered in other institutions and local colleges. Parents develop leadership skills through their roles in the program, by organizing events or other aspects of the program, serving on advisory councils or governance bodies, forming a parent council, or consulting on program development issues.

● Preparing parents to be involved in community-level decision-making on issues they have deemed important. To help parents prepare for a meeting with other decision-makers, staff might brief parents on the purpose and agenda of the meeting, help them to understand the decision-making process, rehearse and role-play with them, and discuss the questions that they will ask. Staff can facilitate parents' attendance at meetings by providing childcare and transportation or by accompanying them.

● Organizing advocacy opportunities. Programs encourage participants to advocate at local, state, and federal levels, and work with them to spearhead activities such as letter-writing campaigns, voter registration drives, and visits to legislators. Programs encourage parents to form coalitions with other groups who share their goals and concerns.

4

Key Practice 4: Promote awareness of and joint responses to community issues among the general public and among other community agencies and institutions.

Community issues and challenges are usually beyond a single program's capacity to address and resolve. Through their work with families and with other agencies, community-based programs form coalitions that can more effectively meet the needs of the community. Important to forming coalitions is building public awareness and consensus around the issues to be addressed. Program staff, in conjunction with parents, provide leadership in raising public consciousness.

Some ways for programs to accomplish this are:

● Using task forces, coalitions, and collaborative groups to advance community issues. Both parents and program staff play active roles in local coalitions and task forces.

● Attending and testifying at public meetings and hearings. Parents and program staff can attend together.

● Forming and maintaining relationships with influential people in the community. Parents, program staff, and members of the program's board of directors may have acquaintances, friendships, and professional working relationships with people who can be helpful in advancing the community's agenda. Programs encourage staff and parents to tap these relationships as sources of influence in advocating for the community.

● Attending meetings on city planning, capital improvements, and budget appropriations at the community level and the state level. Being at the table while these issues are discussed is one way to direct funding and other resources towards community improvements.

● Using the media. Program staff develop relationships with local newspaper, TV, and radio reporters; write op-ed pieces or columns for local newspapers; and agree to be interviewed on public radio stations or cable TV programs. Some programs broadcast public service announcements on public access cable TV stations.

Practice Example

As the director of our community's family center, I always try to keep my ears open for new opportunities to improve conditions for families. One way I do that is by belonging to a couple of national and state-based advocacy groups that keep me informed of new legislation, regulations, and potential funding opportunities. A while back, I received information from the Family Resource Coalition about a new piece of federal legislation that was going to provide funding for prevention and early intervention efforts to my state. The information said that the legislation required the state to include community-level input in deciding how the dollars would be spent, and that the state's child welfare agency was administering the program. In the past, our state's child welfare agency had had very little to do with prevention-focused, community-based programs like ours, so I knew it might take some work to get our foot in the door. Because I sit on the planning committee of our local United Way, that body helped lobby the agency and the governor's office to get some of us included on the statewide planning committee. Once that happened, we campaigned to get parent consumers on the committee and to make it a requirement that any local planning committee also involve parent consumers.

While the planning process didn't go perfectly, we feel it was important just to get to the table—and to get parents to the table. Those voices would have never been heard without our involvement, and hopefully, we have laid the groundwork for further collaboration with this important state agency.

Guideline D: Programs work to develop a coordinated response to community needs.

Key Practice 1: Participate in community-wide planning efforts.

Families require a range of resources and services throughout the community. In order to identify gaps in services and to avoid unnecessary duplication of efforts, community agencies and institutions plan together how they will meet the needs of local families. The planning process also affords family support program staff the opportunity to informally educate others about family sup-

D
1

PROGRAMS IN COMMUNITIES

port principles and practices and to integrate these principles and practices into the community's service delivery system.

Some ways for programs to accomplish this are:

- Convening a group of service providers to identify and address issues of mutual concern. This group may respond to a specific issue that community members have identified as a priority. It may respond to a Request for Proposals (RFP) or apply for a grant.

- Participating in existing efforts to plan new or revised services or programs. Program staff and parents serve on publicly sponsored or privately organized boards, planning bodies, and coordinating councils. Similarly, they attempt to be at the table when planning initiatives sponsored by public agencies or the government are taking place and when community responses to these initiatives are being planned.

- Involving representatives from other agencies in the program's planning process

- Assembling a resource guide or directory of local service providers

Key Practice 2: Collaborate with other community institutions and agencies in tangible ways.

Relationships among service providers are vital to promoting a family support agenda in the community and to helping families access needed services. By collaborating with other institutions and agencies, family support programs provide more opportunities, resources, and services for their participants than they would be able to otherwise. These collaborations make services more accessible to families, who may be close to one organization but far away from another, and can increase cultural awareness and sensitivity by promoting sharing among different groups. Joint activities make all participating service providers more accountable to the needs of families. Even if the actual services provided by a program do not change as a result of collaboration, coordinating efforts does help the community increase the efficiency and effectiveness of its service delivery system.

Some ways for programs to accomplish this are:

- Formally linking the program's efforts with those of other agencies. Some community service providers create a standard intake form that they can all use. Others maintain formal linkage agreements with other programs or agencies. Many programs co-locate with other service providers.

2

Practice Example

Our family resource center provides a variety of services and support to pregnant and parenting teens. Many of the moms involved in the program were having difficulty finding the reliable, affordable childcare that would enable them to stay in school. We responded by starting a childcare program at the center.

After a while, it became to clear to us that this wasn't the best way to meet this particular community need. To run a first-class infant center, you need lots of resources—money, trained staff, additional administrative personnel—things we didn't have in abundance. We decided that if we couldn't run a first-class operation, then we shouldn't run one at all.

We spoke to our city's human services director about the problem. She helped us call a meeting of interested parties in the community—other not-for-profits, representatives from the schools, the local United Way, and many others. Over a period of several months, we worked together to come up with a plan for providing the service. The United Way agreed to provide funding for a local not-for-profit childcare agency to run the childcare program at our center. Since that agency already administers three other programs in the community, they have the providers and staff who are knowledgeable in licensing, regulations, and the like.

Figuring out how best to meet this community need for affordable childcare was sometimes a painful process, especially because there was a short period of time when childcare services weren't being provided at all. But I think we all learned a lot. The process compelled the entire community to take ownership of the problem and to resolve it.

Many programs exchange services with other agencies. For example, one family support program provides job training; another local agency counsels families. The counselors agree to serve ten participants of the job training program in exchange for the job training program taking on ten clients of the counseling program. Programs also collaborate on activities, events, and projects in which all are interested and invested.

- Exchanging information. Programs convene and attend meetings with other local service providers, create and share resource directories, and encourage staff members to talk with and get to know staff from other agencies.

- Sharing or exchanging staff. Staff of different programs collaborate by participating in joint training, interagency teams, and case staffing (where staff members from different agencies work together to address the needs of a particular family).

Key Practice 3: Promote accountability in human services delivery systems that ensures effective services for families.

Since a number of families who participate in family support programs are also involved in other human services systems, family support program staff often hear parents' stories of their experiences—and their frustrations—with these systems. Family support staff directly observe how the rules and regulations governing these systems affect families' ability to access the resources and support they need. These staff are excellent resources to recommend how services can be made more accessible, accountable, and effective.

Some ways for programs to accomplish this are:

- Being involved in legislative advocacy efforts. Programs track legislation that could affect services for the families whom they serve. They develop a legislative agenda and spearhead efforts to advance that agenda.

- Educating program staff about social service system issues that affect the program. Staff participate in planning boards, join state and national task forces dealing with human services change, and connect with national organizations that promote awareness of public policies and practices across the country. Programs subscribe to and encourage staff to keep informed on discussions and directions in human services systems change.

- Increasing telecommunications capacity. Subscribing to an on-line service such as HandsNet or getting direct access to the Internet, allows programs to gather up-to-date information about public policy initiatives, and to respond quickly by downloading letters, creating fax trees, and participating in e-mail campaigns.

Practice Example

Layoffs and downsizing have hit our state hard and unemployment is higher than the national average. As the administrator for our state's network of family resource centers, I've had my hands full trying to maximize our ability to help. Our initiative is a collaboration among three state agencies and the community-based organizations that sponsor centers. The state provides funding to these centers and requires them to provide core family support services such as parent education, on-site childcare, referrals to other community services, and developmental screening for children. Each community has added other components based on its families' needs.

A couple years ago, two of our centers responded to the severe unemployment by working with their local community colleges to provide GED preparation, job re-training, and other employability services at the centers. Since then, we've noticed that rates of participation at these two family resource centers have been consistently higher than those of others. Not only do more people attend; they are involved with the centers for a longer period of time.

As a result, we are doing all we can to bring state and federal dollars for job training and adult education into all of the centers.

3

4

● Encouraging human services systems to enhance their effectiveness by adopting a family-friendly approach. Programs serve as intermediaries to bring parent concerns to service professionals or policymakers. Program staff form collaborative relationships with human services staff, share knowledge that supports positive changes in the system, and emphasize their shared goal of increasing the health and well-being of families and the community.

Key Practice 4: Work to secure adequate resources to support the healthy development of children and families in the community.

Meeting the goal of optimal development and enhanced quality of life for children and families requires that adequate resources be invested in communities. Family support programs work to ensure that all families in their community can meet their basic needs; they understand that families faced with problems such as lack of housing, food, health care, and protection from unsafe and unhealthy conditions may require immediate access to emergency services. To promote the healthy development of children and families, however, programs must go beyond satisfying basic needs; they must intervene in crisis situations and help families solve problems. Programs prevent problems by offering education, resources, and support and by encouraging parents to advocate for public policies and distribution of resources that would afford their family a better life.

Some ways for programs to accomplish this are:

● Designing program components that help parents meet their families' basic needs. Some programs create jobs and hire community members to fill them. Some offer (or collaborate with an agency that offers) job training and classes in trades such as plumbing, carpentry, or electrical contracting; typing; or computer operation. Programs offer access to services that make it possible for parents to provide for their families, such as transportation, childcare, health care, and legal aid. Programs also assist families by developing food and clothing cooperatives and pantries, arranging for emergency loans and financing from community merchants and financial institutions, collaborating with other community institutions in establishing emergency shelters, and linking with local health departments or private health care institutions to provide on-site preventive and health maintenance intervention for families.

● Pursuing funding opportunities that are beyond the traditional scope of the program. Programs look for opportunities to bring money to the community by, for example, expanding the program's scope or being the lead agency in a community development project.

● Building up and beautifying the physical infrastructure of the community. Examples of such projects include installing lights in vacant lots; refurbishing homes that are in disrepair; planting community gardens; initiating clean-up campaigns; and pressuring the city to clean up local parks, fix potholes, or provide the resources to make physical repairs possible. Programs may provide community residents with resources, such as house paint, or bicycles for a neighborhood patrol. Some programs initiate community service projects, such as community policing and anti-drug marches.

● Promoting and creating helping networks such as babysitting co-ops, volunteer banks, and mentorship or apprenticeship programs.

Key Practice 5: Help families to make their voices heard as they advocate for change.

Family support programs help families see new possibilities for themselves and for their communities and programs are natural points of congregation for families to develop community agendas. Some of these may involve nongovernmental actions such as strengthening neighborhood networks of support and engaging in collective efforts to build new community resources. Others may involve changing the way existing systems such as schools, human service agencies, employment and training programs, and housing authorities respond to family needs. Still others may involve political actions to secure more resources for the community (including better housing and more jobs, but also including greater representation in decision making) and to make residents' voices heard at the community, state, and even national levels. Regardless of what specific actions families decide to take to effect change in their communities, family support programs support families' efforts to organize effectively and to maximize their likelihood of success.

Some ways to accomplish this are:

● Encouraging social action. The program does not have to lead or direct advocacy activities; but it can be invaluable in providing a safe and supportive locus where such activities can occur. Programs encourage social action by providing forums for addressing identified social concerns and by networking with other community organizations in+volved in advocacy work and helping parents who express and interest in advocacy to learn about relevant organizing work in the community.

● Supporting families in monitoring governmental programs and assessing community needs. Family support programs can help families build their political skills by providing support and encouragement for those who wish to become involved. This includes assistance in surveying their communities, speaking with other residents, and providing outside monitoring of public programs and practices.

● Providing space for meetings and organizational activities and assistance in organizing meetings and events.

● Representing views, grievances, positions, and demands of program participants before other groups. Some family demands may include changes in school or human service agency practices, and programs can use their existing influence and rapport with those agencies in pressing for such needed changes.

Practice Example

When the families participating in the Brooklyn Family Development Program (BFDP) learned of the city's plan to close two local subway stops due to a budget crunch, they wanted to voice their objections. Many parents took the subway to and from work, and their children took it to the middle school. If the stations closed, many nine- to eleven-year-old kids would have to walk nearly a mile to get home, sometimes in the dark, some through gang territory.

Some parents wanted to surprise the city council at their next meeting by marching in mass, petitions in hand, to demand that service be continued. But at a parent-initiated community meeting held at BFDP others, including BFDP staff, raised questions. Would surprising the council help the parents' cause? What if the council simply needed more information to make the right decision? Were any hearings or public discussions scheduled?

Parents learned of a public forum convened by the city council at which residents could speak. They would tell the city council of their plans to attend, and this would give council members time to search for solutions prior to the meeting.

Families and staff discussed the plan in depth and determined everyone's role in carrying it out. Staff would draft the petitions, parents would visit all their neighbors and gather signatures, and still other parents would make a banner. A letter was drafted to tell the city council of BFDP's intentions. In the process each person learned a lot about the others' strengths and the strategic planning necessary to carry out a grassroots advocacy campaign.

After the meeting, which drew a standing-room-only crowd and attracted media attention, the city decided to keep the busier of the two stops open and to provide a van that would ferry children every school-day morning and afternoon to two locations near the stop which was to be closed. Also, they suggested that the parents submit a proposal for one of the local elementary schools to become part of the citywide Community Schools Program, which would make the school a community center that also offered after-school and weekend activities. BFDP followed the council's recommendation and received funding.

Programs in Communities: Challenges in Practice

1. Funding sources for programs sometimes question the program's role in advocacy activities.

The emerging role of family support services as advocates for systems change is a departure from the practices of more traditional service organizations, which concentrate their efforts on serving individuals. When this difference in approach is not explained, it can cause confusion and difficulties with funders that are accustomed to less advocacy from social service and educational organizations. Family support programs take care to articulate their rationale and methods for working toward change to funders. Few would argue that encouraging families to become more knowledgeable, active citizens, and assisting them in accomplishing this, would be harmful or undesirable.

Occasionally, legal issues arise about the use of funds for advocacy purposes. While the laws that regulate not-for-profit organizations pose restrictions on some political activities, such as supporting individual candidates for office, they impose few restrictions on other kinds of advocacy. They in no way prohibit programs from encouraging families to understand legislative issues that affect their communities and using their own resources to act on these issues. More information about legal restrictions can be obtained from the offices of legislators that represent the program's district and from the Family Resource Coalition. Being knowledgeable about the legal restrictions and clearly articulating the program's advocacy role to both participants and funders should prevent misunderstandings and enable the program to take part in a variety of advocacy activities with families.

2. Sometimes conflicts arise between the program's role as an advocate for families and its position within the system of services that it is trying to change.

Family support programs are increasingly seen as a vital part of the array of resources that should exist in every community. Many state governments have recognized that local, family-directed programs and services are a powerful way to make sure that services are more comprehensive and less fragmented for families. Family support programs often act as coordinators of services for families, and as a result they often have close relationships with public agencies such as those that administer child welfare, health and mental health services. These close relationships with "the system" can cause difficulties in building trust with families who have had negative experiences with public services. It also can cause confusion among staff about their primary commitment: are they advocates for the families with whom they work, or are they allies of the system that provides their paychecks?

Programs cannot increase the integration of services for families without advocating to change policies and practices that are barriers to the goal of comprehensive services. To reduce the conflicts that can arise due to programs' different roles, family support programs make sure that they and any other entities involved in the systems in which they function have clear expectations of their participation. Programs also provide additional training for staff of all types so that they will recognize and take advantage of appropriate opportunities for systems change, and institute mechanisms for review and change that respond to the concerns of local programs. The expectation that family support workers will advocate for families' concerns through systems change should be backed up by the program's full support for staff leadership.

3. The program's efforts to plan and implement collaborative services sometimes are met with resistance from agencies and institutions that are satisfied with the status quo.

Many family support programs are part of new, innovative initiatives that are funded by state or local governments or by collaborative efforts of local businesses, foundations, and United Way chapters. For older, more established public and private agencies, these new collaborations sometimes seem like a threat to their funding and their traditional ways of doing business. In response, family support programs work to build trust with these potential collaborative partners in their communities to overcome initial suspicion and distrust, just as they do with families. They build trust gradually; always keep their promises; and are persistent and flexible.

Some agencies are very resistant and are unlikely to respond to family support programs' efforts to build relationships. The most effective strategy in these cases is often to involve the whole community in the planning effort, so that the family support program itself does not become the target for resistance to change.

Principle Eight
Programs are flexible and continually responsive to emerging family and community issues.

Principle Nine
Principles of family support are modeled in all program activities, including planning, governance, and administration.

Effective family support practice depends on a program environment which integrates family support principles into every aspect of the program's operation. The program's design and implementation over time, their governance and administration, reflect the approach to families and communities expressed in all the other practice principles.

Defining Flexibility and Responsiveness

One of the reasons for the increasing popularity of family support programs among policymakers is their capacity to start where families are and to respond to their needs instead of offering an inflexible set of services. Just as one size of clothing cannot possibly fit everyone's (or sometimes anyone's) body, a single version of family support cannot possibly meet the needs of all of the different families that programs serve. Flexibility means that a program's services are tailored to fit the preferences and needs of the families it serves. Responsiveness means that the program, with input from its participants, continually evaluates what it offers families and changes its array of services in response to their needs.

Flexibility and responsiveness work on two levels: at the staff/family level and at the program design level. The practitioner's responsibility is to respond to families individually, according to their situations and needs. In a home visiting program, for example, a staff member may arrive for a visit with a particular parent-child activity in mind and discover a situation that requires adapting or even abandoning the activity for that day. If a child is ill and the parent is concerned about getting immediate medical attention, the home visitor needs to shift the focus of the visit to address this problem. If there are other children present that the home visitor did not expect, the activity may need to be adapted to include them.

At the program design level, flexibility and responsiveness mean the program's services are evaluated and altered continually as the needs of the families change and as the program learns more about how to work with its participants. For example, a program may be working to provide child development classes, parent-child activities, and drop-in time for parents. If a major employer in the community suddenly closes and a number of people lose their jobs, the ripples of this stressful event will be felt in the lives of the families in the program. The program may quickly find itself organizing relevant resources: job search seminars, budget workshops, stress reduction activities, and support groups. The program's commitment to support the larger community around the program also carries with it the responsibility to change course, shift resources, and respond in a timely way to pressing neighborhood needs. (See also chapter 5.)

The program and the practitioner are interdependent as they implement a flexible, responsive program. The program expects staff to be creative and resourceful in developing relationships with families and in working in partnership with them. The program makes it possible for staff to fulfill that expectation by giving them the authority and resources they need to do their jobs. For example, a staff person may learn that a mother would like to attend the program's afternoon workshops but has no transportation while her husband is at work. The program makes it possible for the parent's needs to be met by allowing the staff member to explore options for solving the problem such as having the program provide money for public transportation; arranging for a staff member, parent participant, or volunteer to provide transportation; changing the time of the workshop; providing the parent with the information through home visits; or other options. If the program does not allow the staff person such flexibility, it becomes impossible for the staff member to do his or her job optimally.

Responsiveness also implies that participating families play a large role in developing a program that is useful and effective to them over time. For example, in a home visiting program with a parent education focus, there should be opportunities for parents to shape the content of the program by developing their own ideas of key activities for the curriculum.

Responsiveness: A Key to Program Effectiveness

In contrast to the categorical service system that has attempted to match families to services, family support programs are designed to respond in a holistic way to the multiple needs of whole families. In working with families in their own neighborhoods, nothing stays the same; in fact, a central purpose of family support programs is to encourage and facilitate families' growth, which inevitably involves change. Family support programs need to respond quickly to what they are learning about their families; if they do not, they risk becoming irrelevant and ineffective. The business literature of the 1990s cautions organizations about the perils of not responding to the changing needs of their customers and consumers. Since family support practice is based on close relationships and functional partnerships with families, programs are well positioned to continuously implement what they learn from their "customers" in their design and administration. Because the built-in flexibility of family support programs results in services that are effective for families in neighborhoods,[1] more and more government initiatives have included community-based programs in their planning and administration of services.

How Programs Model Family Support Principles

Program staff and administrators model family support principles by holding themselves, in their dealings with each other, to the same standards that they set for working with families. Staff are expected to work in partnership with families, encourage families to make decisions, and build families' capacity to advocate for themselves. Similarly, empowerment and capacity building are part of the relationships that staff

and other program leaders develop as they set and carry out administrative policies and procedures. Staff are expected to honor and affirm cultural diversity and to work actively in building new community resources. Likewise, program administration takes place in a setting in which diversity and community building are integral.

All program leaders have a responsibility to create an organizational climate that reflects the principles of family support. When they carry out this responsibility, staff can expect to work in partnership with each other and with other program's leaders, to have support and opportunities to build their own capacity, and to collectively create an atmosphere in which the resources of each person are fully utilized. Programs model internally the kind of diverse, democratic community that they envision as the goal of the larger community. And conversely, the collaborative power sharing in which the program engages outside of its own walls is reflected in its internal workings.

Programs include all stakeholders—participants, staff, board members, funders, and administrators—in their planning of services and the allocation of resources. Inclusive planning and governance requires current, adequate information as well as steps to build the capacity of those involved to make decisions effectively. Family support programs provide these essential elements to all participants in the process.

Programs Practice What They Preach

Essential to a program's integrity is congruence between the principles that govern practice with families and those that govern program management. Staff can't be expected to work with families in ways that follow family support principles if their program's design, policies, and administrative practices and do not support them. While many factors influence how front-line staff work with families, the beliefs about families and their capacity to nurture their children held by the program leadership can have a significant effect on the way services are ultimately provided.[2] The application of these beliefs in the program's administrative policies and practices substantially shape the parameters of staff practice with families.[3] A host of administrative issues—such as staff roles, organizational decision making practices, policies regarding work hours and workloads, training and support available to staff, the mechanisms for evaluating job performance and ensuring individual accountability—can have a dramatic impact on the practitioner's ability to work with families in accordance with the guidelines for family support.

Well-intentioned policies may also have unintended effects. For example, a program whose policy is to hire only registered nurses as home visitors may, in a given area, be unable to fill its home visitor positions with bilingual staff who speak the same language as that spoken by many of the families the program intends to serve. Due to the mismatch, staff and families may have difficulties forming effective relationships, and the program may not have the funds to provide alternative supports that might enable these staff to do their jobs effectively: adequate supervision, interpreters to go along on visits, ongoing cultural competency training, and opportunities for staff members of the language and ethnic background of participating families to work with the others. (See chapters 2 and 3 for more on this topic.)

The participation of families in program governance and program evaluation is part of empowering families in the larger community. By working together to make decisions within the program, staff and families create a learning environment in which parents apply new information and exercise skills that they can use to advocate for themselves. The program itself is a "community learning system"[4] in which everyone participates in the empowerment process. Programs, like individual staff members, act as mediators to build families' capacity to respond to unequal power relationships, such as those created by racism in the larger community, and take initiative to change those relationships. By creating an environment in which families have access to resources and share power, the program can help families who have difficulty doing so believe that change is possible.[5] And there is growing evidence that evaluation results are more valid when program families participate in design and implementation of the evaluation process, and interpretation of the findings. Participation in the evaluation process can also provide an opportunity for program participants to empower themselves, if they are respected as important members of the evaluation team.[6]

A program that demonstrates family support principles in its planning, governance, and administration provides staff and program participants with tangible examples of how to implement these principles in other ways. Theory regarding adult learning has long held that modeling is a powerful tool for adult development, which is a goal of many family support programs. Reinforcing the principles through all aspects of the program sets the stage for consistent, ongoing learning for both staff and families as they pursue the outcome envisioned by all family support programs: promoting healthy functioning for families.

PROGRAM PLANNING, GOVERNANCE, AND ADMINISTRATION

NOTES

[1] Schorr, L. (1991) "Attributes of effective services for young children: A brief survey of current knowledge and its implications for program and policy development." In L. Schorr, D. Both, and C. Coople, eds., *Effective services for young children.* (Washington, D.C.: National Academy Press) 23–47.

[2] Dunst, C. J., C. M. Trivette, A. L. Starnes, D. W. Hamby, and N. J. Gordon (1993) *Building and evaluating family support initiatives: A national survey of programs for persons with developmental disabilities.* (Baltimore, Md.: Paul H. Brookes).

[3] Stoot, F. and J. M. Musick (1994) "Supporting the family support worker." In S. L. Kagan and B. Weissbourd, eds., *Putting families first: America's family support movement and the challenge of change.* (San Francisco, Calif.: Jossey-Bass) 212.

[4] Chavez, M. D. (1994) *About building communities: Connected by our sensitivity and understanding, we form new paths.* (Albuquerque, N.M.: University of New Mexico, Family Development Program).

[5] Solomon, B. "Families and communities: A social policy perspective on diversity." (Unpublished paper).

[6] Whitmore, E. (1995) "Evaluation and empowerment: It's the process that counts." In M. Cochran, ed., *Empowerment and family support.* (Ithaca, N.Y.: Cornell Media) 2 (2), 1-7.

Van der Eyken, W. (1995) "Evaluating the process of empowerment." In M. Cochran, ed., *Empowerment and family support.* (Ithaca, N.Y., Cornell Media) 2 (2), 8-12.

GUIDELINES FOR FAMILY SUPPORT PRACTICE

Program Planning, Governance, and Administration: Guidelines for Practice

While it is natural that most of the energy of a family support program is directed towards its relationships with families, programs realize that relationships among and activities of staff are integral to establishing and maintaining a program that operates in accordance with family support principles. Programs maintain quality by integrating family support principles into all aspects of the program's daily life.

Guidelines and Key Practices

Guideline A: All staff work as a team, modeling respectful relationships of equality.
Key Practices
1. Build a staff team consistent with the program's goals, design, and community.
2. Provide ongoing staff development on the principles of family support.

Guideline B: Supervision and mentorship enable staff members to learn from each other.
Key Practices
1. Establish supervision as a collaborative process.
2. Establish an effective, consistent supervisory system that provides support for all staff members and ensures accountability to participants, funders, and the community.
3. Provide regular opportunities for reflection among staff members.
4. Ensure that there are mechanisms to support staff when problems or difficult situations arise.

Guideline C: Program planning and implementation continually respond to the norms and concerns of the communities and families served.
Key Practices
1. Ensure that the program hires people who are creative and flexible and whose top priority is the well-being of families and children.
2. Ensure that the program is dynamic and that it changes in response to families' and the community's priorities.

Guideline D: The family support program creates a governance structure that institutionalizes its mission and vision and ensures its fiscal health.
Key Practices
1. Structure governing bodies so that they reflect the diverse constituencies of the community and are knowledgeable about community needs.
2. Use formal and informal mechanisms of building consensus on policy issues.

Guideline E: Through their policies and practices, programs promote equality among different cultural groups.
Key Practices
1. Infuse diversity into all aspects of the program.
2. Acknowledge and address inequalities.

Guideline F: Program evaluation is a collaborative, ongoing process that includes input from staff, families, program administrators, and community members.
Key Practices
1. Establish processes and procedures for regularly scheduled evaluation.
2. Ensure that all evaluation procedures—including those used by outside evaluators—are collaborative and involve families and staff from the beginning of the process.

Guideline A: All staff work as a team, modeling respectful relationships of equality.

Key Practice 1: Build a staff team consistent with the program's goals, design, and community.

Family support staff—administrative and front-line, paid and unpaid, full-time and part-time—are key to the program. They are responsible on a day-to-day basis for realizing its mission, vision, and concrete objectives, and for assuring that the program fully integrates the principles of family support into activities and operations. The respect staff extends to families is modeled in the respect and teamwork existing between staff members. Program effectiveness depends on the staff's ability to implement the program goals and design, and to be responsive to the community in which the program is located.

Some ways for programs to accomplish this are:

- Assuring diversity in staff background. Because families are diverse and have different needs and goals, programs have found that they are most effective when their staff members vary in educational backgrounds, areas of training, and life experiences. In all situations, when staff of different backgrounds maintain positive, respectful relationships with each other, they model such relationships for program participants and others in the community.

- Hiring staff who represent the cultures, ethnic backgrounds, and socioeconomic situations of program participants.

- Screening staff carefully. Programs interview potential staff members about their attitudes towards families and their previous work experience in the social services. Many programs involve program participants in the hiring and screening process. Increasingly, programs are looking into the backgrounds of potential staff members to ascertain whether or not applicants have police records, especially those that reflect incidences of child sexual abuse or substance abuse. Many programs screen applicants for drug use.

- Creating opportunities for staff to share diverse experiences. Staff may meet in small teams to talk about their work with specific families, their feelings, and their challenges. Programs may organize a staff team for the purpose of working on specific issues with families. For example, a person with a background in education and a mental health specialist might work together with a family whose child is having difficulty in school.

- Ensuring that the program makes use of the resources and insights that each staff member brings. Programs hold regular meetings and retreats to ensure that staff from diverse disciplines influence all activities and services and to avoid

Practice Example

I never would have been able to be effective with Claire's family if it weren't for the help of my supervisor and coworkers.

Claire needed a lot of support: she was on welfare, didn't have a permanent place to live, had two little ones and was pregnant with her third. Not surprisingly, she was depressed and had low self-esteem. There were so many things to do! She needed better, more consistent prenatal care, mental health counseling, and help with some legal problems. The kids needed to be in an early childhood development program. And the whole family needed a safe place to live.

It was clear that I would have to spend a fair amount of time with Claire and working on her behalf. My supervisor arranged to temporarily reassign some of my other families to others at the center, which is what we typically do for each other in such situations.

GUIDELINES FOR FAMILY SUPPORT PRACTICE

isolation of any individual staff member or group of staff members.

● Ensuring manageable workloads for staff members. The work of family support program staff is to develop and maintain relationships with families. Programs work to reduce staff members' stress level and to regulate the amount of responsibility placed on individual staff members, so that they can develop these partnerships. In instances where staff members are working with families in crisis or with multiple, severe challenges, programs are especially careful to ensure that staff have the time and the resources necessary.

Key Practice 2: Provide ongoing staff development on the principles of family support.

It is easy for family support professionals to accept the principles of family support in theory; it is much more challenging to apply them in practice. Doing so requires continual reflection and attention. Ongoing staff development that is based on the principles encourages the development of respectful, equal relationships among staff members. It helps organizations keep their focus, helps them ensure that they are providing quality services and support to families, and is integral to building teams that affirm and foster diversity.

Some ways for programs to accomplish this are:

● Developing consensus around and commitment to the program's mission and principles. Leaders of a family support program embrace the program's specific mission. They analyze how the program can accomplish that mission using family support principles, and they build this analysis into staff training, supervision, and program management. Staff periodically discuss the ways in which their behaviors and practices reflect family support principles.

● Ensuring that staff development activities are based on the principles of family support. Staff development opportunities include orientation for new staff and discussion of the principles in staff meetings or staff development retreats. The principles are infused into other types of discussions and training as well. Programs understand that staff training is an ongoing part of the work of family support programs.

Guideline B: Supervision and mentorship enable staff members to learn from each other.

Key Practice 1: Establish supervision as a collaborative process.

Supervision within family support programs occurs in the context of respectful relationships that provide advocacy, support, and mentoring for all staff members. Supervision is collaborative in that it involves shared power, clear mutual expectations, and open communication. In the supervisory relationship, power is held mutually although perhaps not shared equally. (For example, supervisors may have authority that supervisees do not, such as the ability to hire, evaluate, and fire staff.) Supervisor and supervisee respect each other's knowledge, past experience, and expertise: over time the balance of power in the relationship shifts, and the authority of the supervisor diminishes as the autonomy of the supervisee grows.[1]

---

[1] The guidelines and key practices on supervision in family support programs rely heavily on *Learning Through Supervision and Mentorship to Support Development of Infants, Toddlers, and their Families: A Source Book*. Emily Fenichel, editor. (Arlington, Va.: Zero to Three) 1992.

Some ways for programs to accomplish this are:

● Establishing clear mutual expectations. Programs are careful to clarify roles and decision-making authority. Generally, supervisors are responsible for managing finances, supporting staff, and evaluating workers' performance to ensure individual and program accountability. Supervisors establish verbal agreements with those whom they supervise which clarify the boundaries and responsibilities of each. They agree on times, methods, and mechanisms for checking in with each other. Programs provide staff members with clear performance standards and personnel policies.

● Considering alternative ways of supervising. Although the traditional supervisory relationship is one-on-one, many programs are experimenting with peer supervision in which team members supervise each other.

● Treating the supervisory relationship as a partnership, analogous to the relationship between family support workers and family members. Staff discuss the similarities and differences between these relationships. Managers and front-line staff openly discuss the issue of power.

● Creating conditions in which information is shared and communication flows freely in both directions and is protected from those outside of the supervisory relationship. Confidentiality and trust foster communication and maximize the effectiveness of supervisory relationships, just as they do relationships between family support workers and family members.

Key Practice 2: Establish an effective, consistent supervisory system that provides support for all staff members and ensures accountability to participants, funders, and the community. Programs use supervisory relationships as vehicles for transmitting core values, helping staff develop their skills and potential, and ensuring quality of services and accountability to stakeholders. Creating supervisory relationships that serve all of these purposes requires resources and consistency. Programs work to ensure that supervisory relationships and the systems that regulate them not only exist on paper, as job descriptions or lines of authority; but in practice, these exist as consistent, reliable, dynamic contexts in which learning occurs.

Some ways for programs to accomplish this are:

● Establishing individual learning plans. Supervisors work with all members of the staff team (including volunteers) to develop strengths-based, future-oriented, individualized plans. These plans focus on the efforts of staff members and the energy they spend, not just on tasks that they are to complete.

● Setting aside time for supervision. Programs devote time to regular meetings between supervisors and supervisees. Supervision is provided in a variety of contexts: face-to-face meetings, program-wide meetings, peer supervision, meetings of staff who are grouped according to function. Supervisors also seek to accommodate staff members' different learning styles.

● Emphasizing reliability. For example, just as families need to be able to depend on family support workers to keep appointments and give them individual attention, so too can staff members expect this of their supervisors.

GUIDELINES FOR FAMILY SUPPORT PRACTICE

● Establishing individual and group goals and clear performance standards and expectations.

Key Practice 3: Provide regular opportunities for reflection among staff members.

Reflection is both the means and the end of the process of supervision. Providing staff with opportunities to process experiences with colleagues helps to prevent burnout, avoid staff turnover, and maintain program quality. It also helps to create an environment in which staff learn from each other. Reflection involves stepping back from the immediate, intense experience of hands-on work and asking questions. Family support workers examine their feelings about the situations they are encountering and the work they are doing with families, and they analyze the decisions and recommendations they've made.

Some ways for programs to accomplish this are:

● Providing opportunities for informal discussion with supervisors. Programs incorporate daily debriefings or weekly wrap-ups into their schedules; staff don't go home feeling that they can't handle what's going on at work. Many programs sponsor annual or semi-annual staff retreats at which staff assess their work with families and with each other, and evaluate their challenges and successes in incorporating family support principles into their work.

● Devoting part of regular staff meetings to reflection. In these sessions, staff members may openly discuss successes and challenges in their everyday work, things they've tried that have worked well, things they would do differently next time. Managers or front-line staff might initiate the discussion, perhaps asking an open-ended question such as "How are we doing on [an aspect of the work]?"

● Keeping a collective diary in which staff can write their reflections and other staff and supervisors can respond. To make this effective, programs establish safeguards to confidentiality. Names are not used, the diary is kept under lock and key, and pages are destroyed periodically.

● Making reflection on staff-to-staff relationships a norm in program operations. Staff of many programs routinely discuss how they have worked together on specific issues or in specific situations.

Practice Example

I haven't worked in the field as long as my co-worker Justine, but I know a lot about families. When I began working at our center, every time I raised an idea for changing something around here or a suggestion for working differently with a particular family, Justine always seemed to put it down and would have dozens of reasons why it wouldn't work or why my suggestion didn't address "the real issue."

When this happened in staff meetings, I felt humiliated in front of my coworkers. I found myself not offering my ideas anymore, in fear of Justine's public rejection of them, I talked with my supervisor, Lourdes. Lourdes didn't let me vent about Justine for too long. It's policy at our center to confront disagreements head on and not to let coworkers gossip or gripe behind each others backs.

Lourdes arranged for the three of us to meet privately. Justine said she hadn't been aware of how she was coming across. She said she really admired my enthusiasm and that she often found it difficult not to play "devil's advocate." Lourdes helped us develop some mechanisms for working with each other: when possible, Justine would respond to my suggestions later and in private and I would seek out Justine's considerable expertise on an issue in advance of a staff meeting.

Key Practice 4: Ensure that there are mechanisms to support staff when problems or difficult situations arise.

When supervisory systems are collaborative, consistent, and effective, they reduce the incidence of conflicts and difficulties. But conflicts and problems occur in any system. One component of supervision and program management is to create mechanisms for dealing equitably with

PROGRAM PLANNING, GOVERNANCE, AND ADMINISTRATION

difficult situations and at the same time contributing to relationship building and staff development. These mechanisms often allow the program to turn conflicts into "teachable moments"—opportunities for staff members to learn and move forward in carrying out their personal work plans.

Some ways for programs to accomplish this are:

● Having an open-door policy. An open-door policy tells employees that supervisors are available to help them solve their problems, whether these problems are work-related or personal. Open-door policies allow staff access to all senior staff members, including the program director. Each staff member is encouraged to come to his or her supervisor's supervisor to discuss issues that cannot be adequately discussed with an immediate supervisor, or if that supervisor does not satisfactorily or fairly answer his or her questions.

● Establishing clear norms and rules for working together as a team. Staff participate in creating norms and rules and in periodically evaluating them. Programs create mechanisms for changing rules that become counterproductive.

● Having a clear grievance procedure to deal with breaches of agreed-upon norms and rules. Grievance procedures could involve having the disputants meet to discuss their areas of disagreement with an arbiter, such as another staffer or a consultant. Such procedures work when employees are demonstrating good faith and are competent to do their jobs. Supervisors end the employment of staff members who demonstrate bad faith or whose skills do not match the requirements of their jobs. The continued presence of such staff negatively affects the program's environment for workers and for families.

● Providing mental health support for staff members. Programs do this through collaborative agreements with local mental health agencies, part-time positions on staff, or contracts with consultants.

Practice Example

Our family resource center, which is part of a Jewish Community Center in the outskirts of an urban area, has a policy that unless childcare or a children's activity is scheduled, parents are responsible for looking after their own kids, but all of our staff members understand that sometimes exceptions need to be made.

Adina, her husband, and their two-year-old twins emigrated from Russia two and a half years ago. Adina works out of her house as a seamstress, and she comes to the J for ESL classes and to the family resource center during drop-in hours to relax, talk with other Russian-speaking parents, and let her children, Sonia and Daniel, enjoy the toys and books we have here. One afternoon when things were pretty quiet, Adina came in with the kids. I knew immediately that something was wrong. She usually pays a lot of attention to her appearance, but today she was without makeup, had dark circles under her eyes, and looked on the verge of tears. She said hello quietly and then sat down with the twins and started to read to them. Daniel shoved Sonia out of the way and she squealed. Adina grabbed Daniel's arm and sharply admonished him. Daniel started to cry. In a hurry, Adina gathered up the children's coats, preparing to leave.

Adina's really proud, and I didn't want to embarrass her by drawing attention to what had happened. But I knew she needed a break from the kids, and I thought she might also like to talk with somebody. Sima, my supervisor and our Russian-speaking family counselor, was in the coffee room. I said, "Adina, I was just about to see if any of the children would like a story. Would you mind if I read to Daniel and Sonia? There's a new pot of coffee in the other room, and it's actually pretty good." Adina had such gratitude in her eyes as she put Daniel's little coat back on the hook and started towards the coffee room. She said only, "That would be very nice."

Guideline C: Program planning and implementation continually respond to the norms and concerns of the communities and families served.

Key Practice 1: Ensure that the program hires people who are creative and flexible, and whose top priority is the well-being of families and children.

In order to be responsive, family support programs first and foremost hire staff members who

GUIDELINES FOR FAMILY SUPPORT PRACTICE

embrace the program's mission with all their heart and who furthermore have a "can-do" attitude. Family support staff achieve responsiveness by being adaptable and by diligently taking a problem-solving approach. Programs achieve responsiveness in part by hiring staff who show these predispositions, and by then providing training on the principles of family support to develop these abilities.

Some ways for programs to accomplish this are:

- Being extremely careful during the hiring process and during periodic staff evaluations to screen for attitudes, values, and beliefs that are compatible with family-supportive practice. Programs recognize that an employment relationship is not necessarily a lifelong commitment: irreconcilable differences between a program and a staff member do occur, and it is best in such cases to sever the relationship.

- Establishing program practices and rules that promote flexibility and creativity. Programs expect staff to operate within clear guidelines, but also leave room for them to experiment and make decisions independently. Programs reward staff members for meeting families' needs in innovative ways and help staff members develop and exercise their own judgment regarding implementation of policies and procedures.

Practice Example

Our neighborhood is home to many newly arrived immigrants from Korea, Taiwan, and elsewhere in Asia. For years, one of the most pressing needs in the neighborhood was for English as a Second Language classes with childcare during the classes. Our center provided both.

We had always prided ourselves in being closely connected to other service providers in the area. However, we got an abrupt reality check when attendance at our ESL classes began to wane. When we investigated, we found out that three other organizations had started providing the same services.

As a staff, we developed a plan to reconnect ourselves with the community. First, we discontinued the classes, because it didn't make sense to keep providing a service when others were fulfilling the need. An advisory group made up of parents helped us identify other unmet needs that we could fulfill. We decided that our staff members would volunteer to sit on the boards of other community organizations to better keep in contact, and that, we would organize informal get-togethers with staff of other organizations so that we could talk and share information.

Key Practice 2: Ensure that the program is dynamic and that it changes in response to families' and the community's priorities.

Programs show responsiveness not only by fostering creativity and flexibility in staff, but by channeling staff's efforts into keeping programs responsive. Family support programs understand that program development is ongoing; it is not sufficient to provide a set of services and program components and refine their delivery over time. A responsive program by definition is one that evolves as the needs and priorities of participating families and the surrounding community change. In order to remain effective and relevant, programs keep abreast of the changing needs of families and communities and use this information as part of ongoing program planning and development. (See also chapters 2, 3, and 5.)

Some ways to for programs to accomplish this are:

- Soliciting input and feedback from all staff, families, community members and other stakeholders in the program. Families and community members participate with staff in regular discussions of the program's effectiveness. As part of their supervision and evaluation processes, programs seek information about consumer satisfaction and parents' input. In discussions among themselves, staff members bring up the concerns and desires of the families with whom they are working. Many programs use advisory councils to elicit information about the needs and desires

2

of participants, since participating families are sometimes reticent to criticize programs in discussions with staff.

● Establishing relationships and communicating regularly with other organizations in the community that provide services to families. Programs spearhead (or participate in) coalitions of service providers that seek to coordinate and avoid unnecessary duplication of their services. Programs collaborate with other agencies when such collaboration would benefit families.

● Creating mechanisms for incorporating information and feedback from stakeholders (staff, participating families, community members, and funders) into discussions of program development. Programs schedule regular meetings to evaluate and revise services and invite all stakeholders to attend.

Practice Example

When our program started ten years ago, in an impoverished inner-city community, school board personnel told us, "You'll never get these parents to participate. Parents here really don't care about education." But we were committed to working with parents as equal partners in assessing community needs and creating services to meet them. We began by knocking on doors, asking parents what they wanted for their children.

Lo and behold, education was their greatest concern: most blamed their own straitened circumstances on a lack of schooling and they worried that their children would also fail in school and thus be doomed to a similar life. They wanted a preschool for the children where parents would feel welcome and could learn about the intricacies of the educational system. From the beginning parents collaborated with staff to develop the curriculum, establish policies, and manage the day-to-day routines. They formed an advisory board, which now has a number of working committees and is directed by a central coordinating committee of parents and staff. They really run the show day to day.

We also have a board of directors comprised of local business leaders, professionals in other agencies, educators, political officials, and people from the media. They have invaluable contacts and networks that we need to raise money for, formulate policy for, and publicize the activities and services that the parents have decided are needed. They also consult on specific questions.

The most gratifying part is seeing our parent advisory board collaborate in the board's activities. Through this partnership, parents gain the skills and self-confidence that make them more effective educators of their children and more influential members of their community. Board members have gained respect for the skills, energy, and contributions of the parents.

> **Guideline D: The family support program creates a governance structure that institutionalizes its mission and vision and ensures its fiscal health.**

Key Practice 1: Structure governing bodies so that they reflect the diverse constituencies of the community and are knowledgeable about community needs.

Governing bodies provide critical leadership for family support programs and require input and guidance from the community's multiple constituencies. Family support programs utilize several kinds of governance structures depending on the program's organizational structure and auspices. The quality of board leadership is directly related to how well board members know and are connected to the community. In order for programs to realize their mission, board members must understand the strengths and needs of the families and the community and have the capacity to assure the program's financial stability.

Some ways for programs to accomplish this are:

● Ensuring that there are people serving on a governing body who have vested interests in the mission of the organization as well as the capacity to access resources, develop policy, and hire appropriate senior administrative staff.

● Creating ways for families and staff to have access to board-level decision-making processes. Programs develop clear decision-making processes and mechanisms through which families and staff will access them. Many programs include families and staff on their governing boards; some specify a specific percentage of parents as a requirement for their boards of directors. Others have groups of parents who are liaisons to the board. In all instances, parents' and staff's access to decision-making channels and processes needs to be clearly communicated to them.

- Establishing advisory councils to inform decision making and ensure responsiveness. In some programs, advisory councils are composed of professionals who consult on specific programmatic issues. Other advisory councils play an active role in implementing components of the program.

- Using parent councils to ensure the program's responsiveness to the families it serves. Many programs have active parent councils which play a major role in program design and implementation, including hiring of staff and day-to-day administration of the program. Parent councils must have authority to make program decisions or they are ineffective and counterproductive for both the program and the parents involved.

Key Practice 2: Use formal and informal mechanisms for building consensus on policy issues.

When staff, families, and other community members participate in consensus decision-making with the program's board of directors, they accomplish two things: they expose the board and themselves to the whole spectrum of opinions, and they arrive at a decision with which all of the people who hold these opinions can live. Consensus building takes time, but the board needs input from those who will be affected by its decisions in order to make effective, responsive decisions on policy and programmatic issues.

Some ways for programs to accomplish this are:

- Clarifying the program's mission and goals through discussions among staff, families, and the board, and building consensus on the program's mission.

- Providing those on the governing board with topical information on an ongoing basis that will enable them to make effective decisions.

- Encouraging the program's staff and leaders to engage in informal dialogue with families and community members. Effective program directors make time to walk around the program and the neighborhood, making face-to-face contact with people and talking with them about their issues.

- Using formal tools to solicit information. Programs use a variety of formal mechanisms such as participant satisfaction questionnaires, focus groups, exit interviews (the results of which are shared with staff and families), committee meetings, and other regularly scheduled opportunities for people to come together to have a say in the program's functioning and planning.

- Sharing information. Programs keep lines of communication open and provide all stakeholders with equal access to information. Information is the most important requirement for consensus and lack of information the most common reason for disagreement.

2

E
1

Guideline E: Through their policies and practices, programs promote equality among different cultural groups.

Key Practice 1: Infuse diversity into all aspects of the program.

Family support programs understand that promoting equality among different cultural groups requires commitment, attention, and vigilance. Truly affirming diversity is not accomplished through one specific component or through hiring one staff person. In hiring staff, developing and administering personnel policies, composing governing boards, designing program components, and even in decorating the agency, family support programs work to infuse diversity into their programs and to model positive relations among different groups. In this way programs contribute to building a multicultural society that is affirming for all its members. (See also chapter 4.)

Some ways for programs to accomplish this are:

● Maintaining a culturally diverse staff and board, with appropriate representation of the groups participating in the program.

● Reviewing personnel policies and practices and decisions made by the program's leadership and governing bodies with all staff prior to implementation.

● Forming relationships with agencies or programs in the community. Programs which serve a single-ethnic population and have staff reflective of that group, may link with a sister program that serves a different cultural group for certain activities.

● Hiring community residents to be on staff. Programs structure training and promotion so that community members who join the staff as paraprofessionals or volunteers can ultimately participate in the leadership of the program.

● Investing time in building effective, strong teams that can effectively communicate and work together across differences in culture, ethnic background, and language.

● Building diversity into program components and activities. Programs strive for diversity even if participants are of a single ethnic group. For example, when children have access to books, toys, and dolls through the program that represent different ethnic backgrounds, cultures, and

Practice Example

I grew up in a neighborhood back East that was pretty much all Black. Of course I had some contact with White folks, but not much experience with anyone else. Now I live with my baby, Imani, in a big-city neighborhood where there are all kinds of people. I moved out here because of my husband's job, but we split up, so now it's just me and Imani. I asked my neighbor about where to get childcare. She took me to the family resource center the next time she dropped her daughter off, and I signed Imani up.

At first it was hard to connect with so many different kinds of people. But I saw that the staff weren't afraid to ask questions. One time this Mexican woman named Carla asked what Imani's name meant. I felt flattered that she'd asked—even though most of my friends back home who helped name her know it means "faith." I think her asking me gave me the courage to ask other women questions when I saw them acting with their kids in ways that seemed really different.

That's one of the things that makes me think that this program is okay. When we talk about situations we're dealing with with our kids, the workers at the center don't tell us the right thing to do. They get us talking about our different ideas. Sometimes it's lively. But it's just like even when another mom will say something I think is strange, we all get respect.

They have a mother-and-baby play group that we like to go to. I can make friends and Imani loves all the attention she gets. Sometimes we play with the dolls and look at the books (it's never too early!)—lots of them show Black people, and even a lot of the dolls look Black. But there are books about Latino families, baby-dolls from Japan, and even board games in other languages for the older kids.

At holidays I really appreciate my girlfriends from the center. They're my family. We don't all celebrate the same holidays, so there are even more occasions to get together. We did Kwanzaa and Christmas last year. This spring we're going to celebrate Buddha's birthday, with a traditional Japanese children's service. How about that!?

experiences, they internalize the ability to get along with others who are different from themselves. When facilitators of discussion groups on parenting issues present and help families talk about different parenting styles and strategies, parents develop appreciation for and understanding of other cultures.

● Modeling positive relationships among people of different backgrounds. Programs build the skills of families of diverse backgrounds to find common ground and appreciate each other and encourage all involved with the program to see differences as differences and not as deficits.

● Creating mechanisms for staff and families to offer feedback on the program's cultural responsiveness.

Key Practice 2: Acknowledge and address inequalities.

Programs that seek to create a community within themselves in which differences are respected and affirmed, and in which cultures are equally valued and appreciated, do more than preach these ideals. They conscientiously speak out against situations of injustice. Addressing inequalities helps programs gain credibility with those who are being discriminated against and fosters equality and positive relationships among different groups.

Some ways for programs to accomplish this are:

● Encouraging staff to identify and protest discriminatory policies, practices, and programs that prevent families from developing their cultures and languages or gaining access to resources. For example, family support program staff advocate for the ability of children to maintain their bilingualism while in the public school system. They also work with individual families to address situations in which they are receiving unequal treatment, advocating for their needs with other service providers or public systems.

● Avoiding relationships with organizations or membership in collaborations that discriminate. Programs do all they can to avoid contributing to institutionalized racism.

● Sponsoring public education forums on issues related to inequality and racism.

● Creating an environment of continuous learning within the program. Programs do not assume that they have solved the problems of discrimination and inequality, but continually strive to become more conscious of ethnocentrism and forms of oppression. Staff members develop knowledge and awareness about discrimination, oppression, and inequality in our society.

● Addressing overtly racist, stereotypical practices, attitudes,

2

Practice Example

As the director of a family support program located in the mountains of West Virginia, I used to be extremely frustrated with my experience hiring paraprofessionals. Most people in this community were born and raised here. While and I and others on staff have lived here for a few years and have worked hard to build trust and relationships, naturally it's easier for a long-time resident to work with some families. That's why we started to hire and train moms who had been participants in our program to work as home visitors, childcare providers, and in other paraprofessional positions.

We would hire and train them and then, in about a year, they would move on. It was frustrating until we began to look at things from a different point of view. We now think of hiring participants as paraprofessionals as a valuable part of the services we provide.

For most of these women, it is their first entry into the job market. With the right kind of support and supervision, we can help them gain the skills and confidence they need to get that second job and climb another rung on the economic ladder. And they, in turn, enrich the program with their invaluable knowledge of the community and the access to families it provides. It's been an exercise in leadership development for both sides.

PROGRAM PLANNING, GOVERNANCE, AND ADMINISTRATION

and incidents quickly and effectively. For example, in addition to promoting attitudes that value diversity, supervisors and staff members do not tolerate demeaning, derogatory, or racist comments that reinforce stereotypes or express disrespect for cultural or ethnic groups.

F
1

Guideline F: Program evaluation is a collaborative, ongoing process that includes input from staff, families, program administrators, and community members.

Key Practice 1: Establish processes and procedures for regularly scheduled evaluation.

Evaluation is the mechanism by which programs remain responsive. By regularly assessing their own performance in relation to their goals, their visions, their missions, their objectives, and the principles of family support—and by making changes in response to these assessments—programs remain focused and effective. Regular evaluation also allows for timely redirection of program resources when needed.

Some ways for programs to accomplish this are:

● Making evaluation an integral part of each aspect of the family support program. Standards for evaluating all program components are included in plans for administering those components. Programs use evaluation methods consistently and regularly and through evaluation measure the goals of the program against its success in meeting these goals. Programs' boards of directors evaluate themselves annually.

● Utilizing a range of evaluation methods to obtain different kinds of feedback and data. Program staff decide the purpose of an evaluation and structure it accordingly. For example, programs may employ focus groups, surveys, discussions, telephone follow-up, rates of return, or word-of-mouth referrals to gain information on the quality of participants' experiences with the program. In order to understand how many people are participating in the program and who these people are on an ongoing bases, staff may collect this type of information day-to-day. To assess the difference a program makes in participants' lives, many programs use pre- and post-service questionnaires or interviews.

● Treating evaluation as learning opportunity. Family support program staff recognize that unexpected or unintended evaluation results can be beneficial. Through these, staff learn about their assumptions and are better able to refine their programs and practices.

● Providing time and resources for evaluation.

Practice Example

Gus was a retired bus driver who was looking for part-time employment. He seemed amiable enough and we thought he would be perfect to drive our van and perform a few needed maintenance chores around the center. But on his second day, it was clear we had a problem on our hands.

Several of our female African American staff members stopped by to complain about him. It seemed that Gus was in the habit of calling African American women "girls." We decided to give him the benefit of the doubt: maybe he just needed "enlightening." I talked to staff and we thought about ways to use the situation as an opportunity to teach someone about the effects of racist or stereotypical language.

At first staff tried teasing and joking to get him to stop. And then, when that didn't work, they tried a more serious, but still positive tone. Still he referred to them as girls.

Next it was my turn. As the director of the program and his supervisor, I told him in no uncertain terms that his use of the word "girl" was inappropriate and that it was hurtful and disrespectful to African American women—staff and participants. He was warned that further violations of our policies would result in his termination.

Although he protested that he never intended to hurt anyone, his use of the word continued after we spoke. I felt that I had no choice but to let him go.

● Building mechanisms in the program's operations for changing course to respond to evaluations and feedback. Programs revisit their program plans in periodic staff meetings or retreats and revise them in response to the result of evaluations.

Key Practice 2: Ensure that all evaluation procedures—including those used by outside evaluators—are collaborative and involve families and staff from the beginning of the process.

2

In order for evaluation results to be helpful in ongoing program planning they must be grounded in a full understanding of the program's mission, vision, and philosophy. This understanding can only come through communication with all stakeholders, including most importantly, families and staff. The participation of families and staff as partners in the evaluation process is integral to family support programs' evaluation processes, and therefore, these partners are involved from the beginning.

Some ways to accomplish this are:

● Making sure outside evaluators understand the principles and practices of family support and the mission and goals of the program.

● Creating opportunities for evaluators to informally talk to and get to know families and staff. Programs have found that getting to know families and staff helps outside evaluators gain an understanding of the importance of relationships to the program's philosophy and practice.

● Involving all stakeholders in evaluation efforts. Prior to initiating a formal evaluation, programs discuss the prospect with participants, staff, and board members, including the need for and purpose of the evaluation, potential roles for them in the process, and alternative procedures. Programs begin evaluation processes with the support, understanding, and participation of all those invested in the outcomes, treating stakeholders as collaborative partners.

Program Planning, Governance, and Administration: Challenges in Practice

1. Funding requirements are sometimes at odds with family support principles.

Family support programs are often obligated to enter into contracts with a variety of funders to get the resources they need for families in their communities. These contracts may specify that the funding is only to be used for specific services or for specific kinds of families who are eligible for assistance because of an identified problem. These requirements are in direct conflict with the family support practice of serving everyone and providing services based on what families need and want rather than on what systems think they should have.

Programs have several alternatives. (1) They can refuse the funding if its requirements present too many barriers to using the funds within the context of the program. (2) They can negotiate with the funders and present a carefully thought-out explanation for their request to change the requirements. In this case, the program may be able to make a case that the purpose of the requirements can be fulfilled within the context of the program's mission. (3) They can carefully budget their funds from all sources to be sure that they use the restricted funds in accordance with the requirements attached to them while serving families who are excluded by those requirements with funding from other sources. In all cases, programs have an obligation to advocate for funding to be used for supporting families in the flexible, responsive way that is described by the principles of family support.

2. Limited resources sometimes challenge a program's capacity to provide what is needed for effective program management in accordance with family support principles.

Most family support programs, like other not-for-profit community organizations, find it difficult to direct sufficient resources toward the planning and management of the organization. Funding services to families is always the top finan-

cial priority, whether the funds come via contracts with public agencies or through private fundraising efforts. As a result, the resources that the program spends on staff development, streamlining administrative functions, technology, and long-range planning are often limited.

Programs can approach this dilemma by zealously budgeting as much as possible for carefully planned infrastructure improvements. When staff have helped develop and claim ownership of a plan for such improvements, ideas about how to implement that plan in spite of resource limitations will naturally follow. Some programs have joined with other programs and agencies to share resources, provide training, and solve problems. Others have reached out to other community resources such as businesses who may be willing to assist. A well developed plan and an articulate argument for its importance in serving families contribute to greater possibilities for getting funding for improvements in program management.

3. Programs sometimes have difficulty assisting parents in fulfilling the role of full partners in program governance and administration.

Parents who participate in family support programs do not come because they want to run the program; they come because they need something from it. Even when the program intends for parents to share fully in making decisions about the program, parents often are reluctant to take on this responsibility. Many parents with young children have little time or inclination to take on major volunteer roles in addition to their family responsibilities. Parents sometimes participate in programs to a limited extent and for a limited amount of time. They do not have a long-term perspective on the program or extensive knowledge of the program's history and purpose.

Programs bear responsibility for creating avenues for parents to participate in meaningful ways in program governance and for breaking down the barriers to an effective parent-program partnership. Some programs do this by providing many different opportunities for parents to participate in shaping the program; they stress that filling out a survey, participating thoughtfully in a focus group, and giving insightful feedback to staff is as important as serving on committees and advisory boards. Other programs provide extensive training and role-playing opportunities for parents to gain the experience and skills they need to participate as equals with professionally trained staff in program planning, governance, and administration. In every case, once the program assumes that parents are really partners, many strategies can emerge for making the partnership work.

4. The participation of paraprofessionals in staffing family support programs can present challenges to program administration.

Hiring people who come from the program's neighborhood is only the first step in tapping the knowledge and skills that community members possess. Programs define the role of paraprofessionals in the program thoroughly during the program's design; those involved in defining this role turn to the research that has been developed in the field. Careful recruitment strategies, appropriate training, and ongoing supervision and mentoring are essential elements in using paraprofessionals to the fullest.

Opportunities for paraprofessionals to develop their skills and take on genuine leadership roles in the program are also critical elements for long-term success. Programs that employ indigenous workers only in low-paid, low-status positions risk losing the credibility among the community and the program effectiveness that hiring these workers intended to produce.

5. Program staff sometimes have difficulty in setting boundaries in their relationships with families.

Family support practice encourages staff to develop supportive, long-term relationships with families that are similar in many ways to lasting friendships. Both kinds of relationship require a commitment to work through difficulties that may arise and to offer support in response to life events that occur as time goes on. Both offer mutual opportunities for learning and growth in an atmosphere of trust. Both generate genuine affection and caring on the part of both family and staff.

Family support program leaders provide thoughtful guidance in situations that call the role of the professional in this relationship into question. When is it appropriate for families and staff to give gifts to one another? Is it appropriate for staff to attend private family events such as birthday parties and weddings? Should families ever be included in a staff member's private life in the same way? Are there certain events or actions that should be "off limits" in the relationship?

Some programs answer these questions with specific policies that govern such situations. For example, a program may make it a policy that staff do not accept gifts from participants, as an indication that no "payment" is expected for the services provided by the program. As part of staff orientation, such a program trains staff to refuse gifts gracefully and to make the reasoning behind the policy clear to families. Other programs make decisions on a family-by-family or event-by-event basis and by taking into consideration all of the different factors that affect the relationship between the staff member and the family. For example, it may be very important that a staff member attend a wedding or graduation for a young mom who has few friends and no supportive family members; attending such an event would show support of and pride in her accomplishment.

6. Successful programs are often started by charismatic leaders. Working to build a program infrastructure that will continue the program once the founder has moved on can be a challenge.

The energy and vision of a knowledgeable, committed program developer are invaluable assets in initiating innovative, responsive programs. This kind of leader is able to attract funding from a variety of sources, inspire staff, and represent the program very effectively to the outside world. The extent to which this leader helps build inclusive, empowered governance and a program climate supported and transmitted by all staff is the extent to which the program can continue to move ahead without the founder.

Guidelines for Family Support Practice is the beginning point for defining excellent family support practice. It is based on the current practices of local family support programs. Family support is being extended, changed, and re-evaluated in these programs every day. Family support premises are being implemented in a variety of settings far beyond local family support programs. Policy changes at the state and federal levels that will have far-reaching impact on family support programs are imminent.

This atmosphere of growth and change holds great promise for the future of family support. It is a critical time to tell the success stories that family support offers: Many, many families are making it, in their own ways, in their own communities, through the assistance of empowering, common-sense services. Families are getting better, and children are getting opportunities for healthy development. These stories, which are happening every day in hundreds of programs around the country, represent the beginnings of a national commitment to families for which the family support movement has struggled hard.

There are four key arenas in which this commitment can grow: practice, training and education, research and evaluation, and public policy. *Guidelines for Family Support Practice* has a role to play in each of them.

Using Guidelines for Family Support Practice in the Field

Guidelines for Family Support Practice was written for practitioners, those staff members who are working every day in family support programs. The suggestions and strategies in this document came directly from their experience in the field. The book should be used as a basis for setting standards for and expectations of how staff and programs carry out their daily work. The guidelines sections of the practice chapters (chapters 2 through 6) are designed to be used as check lists; every program should be following each of the key practices, using the recommended strategies that fit that program.

Many programs will review these guidelines chapter by chapter as a form of staff development, to assess how their practice measures up to the standards that have been articulated by the rest of the field. The first step is a thorough reading and discussion of the introduction to family support, found in the first chapter. Are the premises familiar? Is there agreement with the fundamental ideas behind family support? What do the principles mean in the context of the individual program? The premises and principles have been edited extensively by many family support practitioners with the goal of eliminating ambiguity. Each phrase included in the principles describes an important idea behind daily practices. Examining each principle and premise in depth is a key element of understanding or, for long-time practitioners, introducing a new perspective on family support practice.

A recommended process for using *Guidelines* in staff and program development is to discuss the practice chapters one by one. Discussion of each chapter should begin with general discussion on its first section, which describes the rationale behind the principles covered in that chapter, so that every staff member is familiar with the theory and research from which the practices emerged. Then the key practices should be discussed in detail so that staff have a chance to understand the meaning of the guidelines and to reflect on how the key practices are carried out in their own programs. Examples and strategies in *Guidelines* may substantially reflect current practice in the program, or they may stimulate immediate changes. The challenges described at the end of each chapter may stimulate further discussion on particular topics or direct attention to nuances of practice that may not come through clearly in the guidelines. When concluding the discussion of each chapter, it is important to review, noting areas in which improvements need to be made, further research and reading are needed in order to clarify points over which there has been disagreement or confusion, and specific training needs to be designed and carried out.

Guidelines for Family Support Practice is designed to be a "living document," part of an ongoing process of refining family support practice. In the course of staff discussions about *Guidelines*, disagreements, suggestions, and challenges are sure to arise. The Family Resource Coalition welcomes comments and suggestions about this document as well as other aspects of practice in the field. These will form the basis for revisions and refinements of the guidelines.

Training and Education for Family Support Workers

Guidelines for Family Support Practice is a statement of what family support programs have found to be effective practice with families over many years. It is not intended to be a tool that, used on its own, imparts the knowledge and skills that staff need in order to carry out effective practice. Extensive training for staff, in their specific jobs and in the practices outlined in this book, is necessary in order for good practice to be a reality in programs. New, comprehensive strategies for both pre-service and in-service training need to be developed based on this book; it also can be used to evaluate existing training curricula for consistency with family support principles.

Most training of family support workers is currently done on an in-service basis. *Guidelines* provides a comprehensive listing of the practices expected of workers; training staff so they can effectively carry out these practices should be a primary goal of programs. Effective in-service training should include adequate skill building for individual staff members as well as team building and team training to allow staff to develop the relationships necessary for working together. Training is often one of the last "luxuries" to be incorporated into a program as resources are allocated, but lack of adequate training is the biggest barrier to full implementation of good practice. *Guidelines for Family Support Practice* can be used to help programs and funders understand all of the dimensions of effective practice and the critical role of training in program effectiveness.

For some key aspects of family support practice, such as the basic relationship between families and workers, training may concentrate on unlearning attitudes that have been developed in other professional training. Professionals are often taught to take charge of situations and focus on diagnosing and fixing problems. Family support calls for the development of a partnership in which the professional is not in charge but rather is a resource or facilitator for families to use on their own terms. Shifting into a different role, with differ-ent goals and expectations, requires the staff member to develop new knowledge and skills as well as to experience personal growth and undertake ongoing reflection. Training that allows for these elements is essential to practitioners' development of capacity for effective practice.

Guidelines is a valuable outline of necessary practices that could be used by colleges and universities as they develop or consider developing curricula for students interested in family support as a career. Pre-service training is already available in some of the areas of practice needed for successful family support work. Schools of social work, for example, offer training in empathic listening, conflict resolution, and creative confrontation with clients, which are important elements of good family support practice. Some schools of social work are beginning to offer a concentration in family support as part of their overall curricula. Some universities offer students opportunities to develop the understanding and skills necessary for collaboration across disciplines, which is another element of good family support practice. Others incorporate family support ideas and practices in several different majors, such as child development, education, and health.

Research and Evaluation

The family support practice outlined in *Guidelines* is based on theory and research in early childhood and family development, community development, social networks, empowerment strategies, self-help, and the impact of racism on child development. Pioneering research in these fields needs to be followed by further research in a number of areas, particularly the interaction between family and community life, families' willingness to seek assistance in child rearing, the family assets necessary for healthy child development, and the psychological underpinnings that children and adults need in order to feel that they have power in their own lives. Basic research in these areas will facilitate further development of the forms of intervention and support that family support efforts should provide.

Family support programs have posed challenges to evaluators from these programs' inception. The unique mix of services and support offered by each program and the usual practice of allowing parents to choose what they need from a menu make it difficult to determine exactly what each participant gets from a program. The many variables that affect family and community life make it difficult to determine what impact a family support program has on an individual child or parent, apart from other influences. To date, most evaluations of program models have focused on changes in specific behaviors or gains in information that are rather easily measured. Few have attempted to discern the overall impact of program activities on child development, family functioning, or community well-being. Questions about program effects are becoming more pointed as more and more resources are directed toward comprehensive family support approaches. The need for creative, insightful evaluation of programs' effects on children, families, and communities is greater than ever before.

Guidelines for Family Support Practice sets parameters regarding what good family support practice includes, thus offering evaluators a place to start in determining whether programs consistently are offering their services appropriately. These parameters emerged from long-term experience in the field and are based on practitioners' best estimates of what has been be successful over time. It remains for evaluators to test these estimates to determine if the practices as outlined here are actually the most effective strategies for reaching the goals programs have set for themselves. These evaluations of program efficacy can then be used to set standards for programs.

Public Policy That Supports Good Practice

Faced with escalating budgets for compensatory, remediation, and protective services, entrepreneurial policymakers have begun to explore new ways of doing business using family support as a strategy for reforming public services for children and families. Studies on what makes public services effective show that current services need to take on many of the attributes of family support programs, which are described in detail in *Guidelines for Family Support Practice*, to

achieve the results they are expected to produce. Infusing family support values and approaches into public health, public welfare, education, child welfare, mental health, juvenile justice, and all other systems that serve families would dramatically and positively change the way teachers teach, child welfare workers protect children from harm, and mental health professionals work with families.

Redesigning services to reflect a family support approach is crucial to the success of these reformed services. New and closer partnerships must form between state and local entities and between public and private funders, and many stakeholders must be involved in decision making in a sustained way. Front-line workers will need greater flexibility and authority than they now have and new training in how to use them effectively. Local planning and governance boards will need substantial preparation to take over new responsibilities. Families who use public services will be involved in governing and planning them in ways that will require new preparation for both families and service providers.

New principles for practice in these public systems should be built from the principles described in this book, with special attention to the ways in which they can be effectively adapted for use in systems accustomed to using standardized prescriptions for services. There is a need for a definition of "best systems," based on family support practice, that will guide these large systems as they work toward family support. There is a need for model legislation and model regulations to guide policymakers in making sure that new laws and programs make excellent family support practice possible. *Guidelines for Family Support Practice* gives a clear picture of what good practice is; policies should be examined for their consistency with both the principles and the elements of good practice delineated here.

The Future of Family Support

The ideas behind family support programs have moved very quickly into the mainstream of human services, community planning, and public policy. They are not especially new ideas, although they are based on new theory and research about children and families. They are not particularly complicated ideas, although changing traditional ways of thinking and working in large institutions can be complicated. The ideas behind family support are more like old-fashioned common sense.

Children thrive when their families are able to provide loving care and adequate necessities like medical care and education. Families do well when they can provide for their children and serve as valued and respected members of their communities. Communities improve life for everyone when there is informed, concerted, active participation in addressing the issues that affect community members.

Family support represents a common-sense commitment to our families and communities that can make a difference for all of us. To make its vision a reality for our country will require effort and commitment from every parent and every practitioner and every policymaker who believes that families are worth supporting. *Guidelines for Family Support Practice* is a first step in articulating how this new national commitment can look in practice.

Affirming Children's Roots: Cultural and Linguistic Diversity in Early Care and Education.
Chang, H. and L. Sakai (1993, San Francisco: California Tomorrow).

* **America's Family Support Programs: The Origins and Development of a Movement.**
Kagan, S. L., D. R. Powell, B. Weissbourd, and E. F. Zigler, eds. (1987, New Haven: Yale University Press).

* **The Basics of Family Support: A Guide for State Planners (and Others).**
Goetz, K. and S. Peck, eds. (1994, Chicago: Family Resource Coalition).

* **Beyond the Buzzwords: Key Principles in Effective Frontline Practice.**
Kinney, J., K. Strand, M. Hagerup, and C. Bruner (1994, Falls Church, Va.: National Center for Service Integration).

Building Communities From the Inside Out.
McKnight, J. (1994, Chicago: ACTA Publications).

* **Building Strong Foundations: Evaluation Strategies for Family Resource Programs.**
Littell, J. H. (1986, Chicago: Family Resource Coalition).

* **Building Villages to Raise Our Children.**
(1993, Cambridge, Mass.: Harvard Family Research Project).

Designing and Managing Programs: An Effectiveness-Based Approach.
Kettner, P. M., R. M. Moroney, and L. L. Martin (1990, (Thousand Oaks, Calif.: Sage Publications).

* **Drawing Strength From Diversity: Effective Services for Children, Youth, and Families.**
Leong, C. and D. De La Rosa Salazr (1994, San Francisco: California Tomorrow).

* **Empowerment and Family Support.**
Cochran, M., ed. (1995, Ithaca, N.Y.: Cornell Cooperative Extension).

* **Empowerment Evaluation: Knowledge and Tools for Self-Assessment and Accountability.**
Fetterman, D. M., S. J. Kaftarian, and A. Wandersman, eds. (1996, Thousand Oaks, Calif.: Sage Publications).

* **Enabling and Empowering Families: Principles and Guidelines.**
Dunst, C., C. Trivette, and A. Deal (1988, Cambridge, Mass.: Brookline Books).

* **Essential Allies: Families as Advisors.**
Jeppson, E. S. and J. Thomas (1995, Bethesda, Md.: Institute for Family-Centered Care).

Evaluating Family Programs.
Weiss, H. B. and F. H. Jacobs, eds. (1988, Hawthorne, N.Y.: Aldine).

* **Families as Nurturing Systems: Support Across the Life Span.**
Unger, D. G. and D. R. Powell, eds. (1991, New York: Haworth Press).

* **Getting Men Involved: Strategies for Early Childhood Programs.**
Levine, J. A., D. T. Murphy, and S. Wilson (1993, New York: Scholastic).

* **Know Your Community: A Step-By-Step Guide to Community Needs and Resources Assessment.**
Samuels, B., N. Ahsan, and J. Garcia (1995, Chicago: Family Resource Coalition).

Learning Through Supervision and Mentorship to Support Development of Infants, Toddlers, and Their Families: A Source Book.
Fenichel, E., ed. (1992, Washington, D.C.: ZERO TO THREE / National Center for Infants, Toddlers, and Families).

A Matter of Commitment: Improving Results for Children, Youth, and Families, A Comprehensive Guide to Ideas and Help (Volumes I & II).
Center for the Study of Social Policy, Child and Family Policy Center, Family Resource Coalition, Center for Youth Development and Policy Research/Academy for Educational Development (1996, Washington, D.C.: Center for the Study of Social Policy).

* **New Expectations: Community Strategies for Responsible Fatherhood.**
Levine, J. A. and E. W. Pitt (1995, New York: Families and Work Institute).

117

* **Putting Families First: America's Family Support Movement and the Challenge of Change.**
Kagan, S. L. and B. Weissbourd, eds. (1994, San Francisco: Jossey-Bass Publishers).

* **Raising Our Future: Families, Schools, and Communities Joining Together.**
A handbook of family support and education programs for parents, educators, community leaders, and policy makers (1995, Cambridge, Mass.: Harvard Family Research Project)

* **Realizing a Vision for Children, Families, and Neighborhoods: An Alternative to Other Modest Proposals."**
Bruner, C. (1996, Des Moines, Iowa: Center for the Study of Social Policy).

* **Supporting and Strengthening Families: Methods, Strategies and Practices.**
Dunst, C. J., C. M. Trivette, and A. G. Deal (1994, (Cambridge, Mass.: Brookline Books).

* **Understanding Latino Families: Scholarship, Policy, and Practice.**
Zambrana, R., ed. (1995,Thousand Oaks, Calif.: Sage Publications).

* **Understanding Race, Ethnicity, and Power:The Key to Efficacy in Clinical Practice.**
Pinderhughes, E. (1989, New York: The Free Press).

* **Within Our Reach: Breaking the Cycle of Disadvantage**
Schorr, L. B., & Schorr, D. (1988, New York: Doubleday).

* **Working with African American Families: A Guide to Resources.**
Ash, C. (1994, Chicago: Family Resource Coalition).

* denotes resource is available from Family Resource Coalition, 200 S. Michigan Ave., 16th Floor, Chicago, IL 60604, 312/341-0900 (phone), 312/341-9361 (fax)

As family support programs have developed throughout the country, a pressing need to define quality in family support practice has emerged. This need is most clearly recognized in the areas of training family support program staff and implementing quality family support programs. In 1991, a group of leading practitioners and scholars of family support gathered at a Wingspread conference convened by the Family Resource Coalition with the support of the Johnson Foundation, Inc., and the A. L. Mailman Family Foundation. The Wingspread participants called for the Family Resource Coalition to take the lead in developing a statement of best practices in family support. In January 1993 the Coalition begin the work involved in producing this statement with funding from the Annie E. Casey Foundation, after a six-month planning period supported by the A. L. Mailman Family Foundation, and the Best Practices Project was born.

The project began with a vision of meeting the need for better definition and articulation of what constitutes best practices in family support programs. It was guided by an approach that drew upon the premises of family support (see appendix C). This approach emphasized an inclusive, participatory process; widespread outreach to diverse communities, programs, and practitioners; a balance of leadership and participation between practitioners and scholars; and careful attention to gathering as much of the relevant information as possible to build a solid base of knowledge in family support.

These guiding values permeated every aspect of the project and were carefully safeguarded throughout its life. They were reflected in the selection of the Best Practices Project Steering Committee; specialized outreach to and networking with diverse and underrepresented groups; the involvement of new programs, practitioners, and scholars; the commissioning of "new knowledge"; and ongoing dialogue among all of the stakeholders in both the process and the outcomes of the Best Practices Project.

This appendix summarizes the various steps undertaken by the project to develop a definition of quality in family support practice. It also attempts to convey some of the insight gained during each step of the unique process and to illustrate that, as family support programs know, a respectful and inclusive process is just as important as outcomes.

A Living Statement

From very early in the Best Practices Project's development, *Guidelines for Family Support Practice* was envisioned as a "living document" that would reflect the dynamism and responsiveness to emerging trends that characterize family support programs and practices. Although the process of carrying out the Best Practices Project was to be as comprehensive, far-reaching, and participatory as possible, it was assumed that *Guidelines for Family Support Practice* would need to be both definitive and dynamic in its statements about quality. As new examples of the strengths, needs, and issues facing families are identified, new examples of best practices will emerge.

Project Objectives

The Best Practices Project envisioned by the Wingspread participants in 1991 was to encompass the theoretical and practical aspects of knowledge and experience deemed necessary to develop a quality family support program. Wingspread participants had many expectations of the statement that was to become *Guidelines for Family Support Practice*; the core of these was that it would articulate the characteristics of a quality family support program and clearly apply the family support principles to practice. The objectives of the Best Practices Project were:

1. To synthesize and make easily available to the family support field and the general public the knowledge and experience of a wide spectrum of family support practitioners, scholars, and advocates

2. To identify and clearly articulate the characteristics of a quality family support program and to illustrate examples of best practices within a quality family support program

3. To develop a diverse constituency of practitioners, families, advocates, scholars, funders, and policymakers that

would support the widespread use of the statement of best practices as a basis for program development, training and evaluation, professional education, and policy making.

Wingspread participants called for a process that mirrored the principles of family support—valuing inclusion and participation, recognizing and supporting the voices and experiences of families and practitioners in the field, and committing to the fundamental goals of empowerment and responsiveness to cultural diversity that are central to family support practice. The goal of producing a living statement that responds to emerging strengths, trends, and needs in family support practice has guided the Best Practices Project.

Project Leadership

A national steering committee of leading practitioners, scholars, funders, and advocates was established to guide the Best Practices Project (see the preface of this book for a list of steering committee members). The Best Practices Project engaged participants and reached out to involve and respond to the people who, it was thought, would use *Guidelines for Family Support Practice*: program personnel and managers, parents, trainers, evaluators, academicians, and policymakers. The steering committee included representatives from these groups. The committee was co-chaired by FRC President Bernice Weissbourd and Douglas Powell of Purdue University. In addition to guiding and informing the process, the steering committee served as the final arbiters of the statement.

The steering committee met twice as a group. Smaller groups and individual steering committee members worked many hours in telephone conference calls, correspondence, review of materials and drafts, analysis of focus-group responses, outreach to broad segments of the national family support community, and ongoing guidance to project staff.

The Process

The Best Practices Project Steering Committee endorsed the following plan for realizing the project's objectives:
1. Thorough search for and critical review of relevant theory

and research
2. Wide-ranging consultation with practitioners and families to expand understanding of how family support principles are being put into practice in a variety of settings and in diverse communities
3. A commitment to an inclusive, open, participatory process for input and feedback from groups of practitioners, families, scholars, and advocates in the field

Identifying the Universe of Family Support Programs and Practitioners

Recognizing that the Coalition's original database did not necessarily capture the universe of family support programs, attempts were made to expand FRC's networks. The Coalition wrote letters to people and programs on the database requesting names of additional programs and people to contact. Other national organizations and public entities were tapped to broaden the outreach effort. The project benefited from increased access to channels of communication through various computer networks.

Special outreach efforts targeted groups that had been underrepresented within the family support network. The Coalition's African American and Latino caucuses played critical roles in expanding the network to these constituencies. Members of the Best Practices Project Steering Committee consulted extensively with project staff to identify programs and practitioners that served Asian and Native American populations. Mailings and follow-up efforts were made to invite diverse groups to participate in the Best Practices Project.

Outreach efforts were also made to ensure a balance of participation from various geographical areas of the country; from urban, rural, and suburban programs; and from programs that serve populations of various socio-economic backgrounds. The institutional auspices or setting of each program was also considered in order to assure representation of independent, community-based family support programs as well as those sponsored by schools, health and mental health care institutions, childcare and child welfare programs, and other public entities.

Developing a Strong Base of Knowledge

Understanding the multidisciplinary nature of family support, the Wingspread participants called for the Best Practices Project to combine family support principles with appropriate knowledge from other fields and disciplines. The intention was that the project would synthesize and analyze the theoretical, practical, and experiential bases of knowledge.

One of the first challenges of the project was to identify the potential sources of literature on family support. FRC requested literature such as staff development manuals and curricula, parent education curricula and materials, program evaluations and reports, newsletters, and other publications from the extensive constituency base developed by the Best Practices Project.

Staff searched traditional sources of literature from fields and disciplines that contribute to family support (social work, education, developmental disabilities, early childhood education, marriage and family studies, ethnic and race studies, psychology, and others). Searching databases proved difficult because the term "family support" as those in the field understand and use it is not recognized in the broad social science literature.

The initial searches produced several hundred references. The publications and dissemination networks created by the family support movement itself, such as the Coalition's own National Resource Center for Family Support Programs, proved to be some of the richest sources of information about family support programs and practices.

A noteworthy problem that surfaced was the scarcity of literature on how family support was developing in African American, Latino, Asian, and Native American communities and in multicultural settings. Again, holding firm to the project's commitment to widespread outreach and inclusive process, the Best Practices Project staff began exploring lesser-known and nontraditional centers of culturally specific knowledge.

Three specific benefits were obtained through this effort: (1) the message of family support was communicated to a wider audience of scholars and practitioners linked to diverse constituencies, (2) lesser-known literature of potentially great benefit to family support was identified, and (3) new leadership emerged from diverse networks of scholars, practitioners, and others who influence both practice and policy.

Research on Special Topics

The Best Practices Project Steering Committee identified four critical areas of family support in which additional research and documentation were needed. These four areas have been the focus of papers commissioned by the Family Resource Coalition. The four papers are:

1. *Best Practices in Community-based Family Support Programs: Key Characteristics and Features*, by Carl Dunst, Allegheny-Singer Research Institute. Funded by the Carnegie Corporation of New York.

This paper integrates and synthesizes current thinking in the field of family support. Dunst articulates a theoretical framework and common program parameters that serve as a useful context for discussing and determining best practices.

2. *Linking Family Support and Child Care: Issues, Experiences, and Opportunities*, by Mary Larner, National Center for Children in Poverty. Funded by the Carnegie Corporation of New York.

Larner undertakes a detailed review of demonstration projects and current two-generation programs, and gleans compelling lessons about the way we structure and deliver services to families.

3. *Community-based Family Support Centers: Working with Abusive and At-Risk Families* (working title), by Joyce Thomas, Center for Child Protection and Family Support. Funded by The Edna McConnell Clark Foundation (forthcoming).

The paper will investigate (1) best practices in primarily voluntary and preventive community-based family support programs working with families reported to child protective services and mandated to participate in parent education or other services provided by the program and (2) how programs serve families at high risk of abusing or neglecting their children (who have not yet been involved with the child welfare system).

4. *Cultural Democracy in Family Support Practice*, by Makungu Akinyela, Ujamaa Family Life Project. Funded by the Charles Stewart Mott Foundation (forthcoming).

This paper will identify a theoretical framework for understanding the issues and relationships that characterize this culturally diverse society, especially as they relate to the field of family support, and will explore the practices of family support programs that serve specific cultural or multicultural populations.

Each commissioned paper takes a scholarly approach to the review and analysis of the literature within a specific family support domain. The papers contribute to the knowledge base of the Best Practices Project but do not necessarily represent the view or final conclusions of the project.

Widespread Consultation With Practitioners

In spring 1993, the Coalition used its expanded database to solicit widespread participation by diverse programs in focus-group discussions. The discussions, conducted throughout the country, were one of the project's primary mechanisms for hearing directly from practitioners and families participating in family support programs.

Plans for the focus-group process reflected the inclusive, participatory nature of the project. Rather than conduct a manageable number of focus groups and have them facilitated by project staff, the Best Practices Project Steering Committee decided to open the process to any program that was willing to follow its guidelines for facilitation and documentation.

With the help of a marketing research consultant, the project staff first developed a discussion guide that consisted of thirteen statements of principle that were based on the principles of family support promoted by the Family Resource Coalition, which at that time numbered five. The project staff developed guidelines for facilitation and documentation and circulated them with the discussion guides. Separate discussions guides were developed for staff focus groups and for family focus groups.

The focus-group discussion guides and facilitation materials underwent many stages of review and revision by both Best Practices Project staff and steering committee members. The materials were field-tested and translated into Spanish. During the period of heaviest focus-group activity, project staff provided technical assistance to more than 100 programs that were sponsoring focus groups.

The Best Practices Project invited approximately 3,000 programs to hold focus groups. Despite efforts to streamline the process, preparing for, conducting, and documenting focus-group discussions placed great demands on the time and resources of programs. Given these demands, one of the project's biggest surprises was the overwhelming response of programs throughout the country that wished to conduct focus groups.

Initially, more than 300 programs agreed to conduct focus groups; 210 focus-group sessions were conducted throughout the United States and Canada by March 1994. With an average of five people per focus group, more than 1,000 practitioners and family members participated in focus-group discussions.

A major by-product of the focus-group process was the overwhelmingly positive enthusiasm communicated to the Family Resource Coalition about the value of the discussion process itself. Programs used the focus groups as opportunities for reflection and self-assessment, staff development, and support and validation of their work. Many programs reported using the results of family focus groups as a way to learn about the successes and shortcomings of their programs. Below are some of the comments offered by programs that participated in the focus groups:

"The experience was extremely empowering, motivating, and energizing for staff. The session provided participants with additional ideas for activities and ways to make their programs more effective. ... Questions in the focus-group discussion were helpful to evaluate their program and set goals for effective growth. Most important thing learned:

There is always hope."

"We are so busy we seldom gather lately, so we enjoyed getting together. ... We learned a great deal from this experience—both about the program implementation and philosophical approaches."

"[Staff] enjoyed the process—we discussed doing a similar process with other staff and with parents. [The] process clarified staff beliefs—brought staff together philosophically. Some of the best learning comes from discussion like this."

"It was reaffirming for staff to look at our program and feel so good about what we do and how we do it."

"It was one of our best and most rewarding sessions ever. I believe our volunteers felt valued once again, and others who were not available were disappointed that they couldn't attend."

"The group's interactions were open, honest and animated! It gave our staff a unique opportunity to discuss issues and share ideas."

"Sometimes I feel we get stuck on our lingo and pat answers and fail to really talk deeply about issues—these questions helped move us towards that, but we've a ways to go yet."

Programs and practitioners value opportunities to reflect, discuss, and gain validation as well a perspective on their work. Practitioners and families have responded positively to a process that reflects the empowering, inclusive philosophy that is the foundation of family support—demonstrating in a tangible way that each participant is a valued resource to the whole.

Profile of Programs Participating in Focus Groups

A total of 210 focus-group sessions were held nationwide; of these, 168 were sponsored by single programs or agencies. Of the single-program focus-group sessions, 93 involved only staff of programs. An additional 75 single-program focus groups were conducted with family participants (see Table 1 for a breakdown of types of focus groups). Inviting families as well as staff to participate in focus-group discussions reflected the value of staff/family partnership that is fundamental to the family support approach. It also provided a way to develop a total picture of a particular program from the perspectives of both staff and participants.

Another 42 sessions were sponsored by programs that collaborated in groups of two or more to conduct focus-group sessions. Reports from most of these sessions included demographic information only on the host or convening agency. Consequently, demographic information on other participating programs was unavailable. For this reason, the following profile of programs that participated in the focus-group process is based on a subset of sessions run by single programs, which totaled 94. (Tables included at the end of this appendix profile the geographic locations, types of community, program settings, racial/ethnic compositions, and economic levels of the populations served, and other characteristics of these 94 programs).

- Geographic region: The Midwest, Southeast, Northeast, Northwest, and Pacific areas of the country (in order of highest to lowest) provided the bulk of focus-group returns (see Table 2). Relatively fewer returns came from the Mid-Atlantic and Southwest regions.

- Type of community: Of the programs that provided data on setting, 65 percent indicated that they served predominantly urban, mega-urban, or mixed settings. However, rural and suburban programs were well represented (see Table 3).

- Program setting: The majority of programs that responded indicated that they were "community-based centers" or "social service agencies," or listed "homes of families" as the primary sites of their work with families. Schools and child-care centers were also well represented, as were churches or synagogues and hospitals or clinics (see Table 4).

- Economic levels of population served: Of responding programs, 44 percent indicated that they served populations that were at or below the poverty level. An additional 29 percent served mixed-income populations (see Table 5).

- Racial/ethnic breakdown of population served: Of programs in which a particular racial/ethnic group represented 50 percent or more of the population served, 56 percent were Caucasian, 14 percent were African American, two percent were Asian, and one percent were Latino. No programs reported serving a population of which 50 percent or more were Native American (see Tables 6a & 6b).

Selection of Questions for Focus-Group Discussions

The focus-group discussion guide included a list of 13 principle statements that were based on the principles of family support, which at that time numbered five. Since it was anticipated that focus groups would not have enough time to address all 13 statements, programs were asked to select five statements for discussion. The choices of questions made by programs are in Tables 7 and 8.

Principle statements that were responded to by 50 percent or more of the 93 staff focus-group sessions included (see Table 7):

- Building on family strengths
- Confident and competent parenting
- Staff and family members are partners
- Services for all family members
- Parent education
- Programs as bridges between families and other resources

Topics that were underrepresented (32 percent or less) as choices for staff focus-group discussion included:

- Parents as program decision makers
- Families as resources
- Parents as advocates
- Cultural respect and diversity; program is community-based
- Voluntary participation in programs
- Staff development and training
- Program effectiveness and evaluation

Questions responded to by 50 percent or more of the fami-

ly focus groups were (see Table 8):

- Building on family strengths
- Seeking support as a family strength
- Confident and competent parenting
- Staff and family members are partners
- Parent education

The areas with fewer responses appear to represent some of the cutting-edge issues that family support programs struggle to address in practice. Some of these areas were identified early in the Best Practices Project and are addressed by commissioned papers, such as the issues of voluntary versus mandated programs and cultural diversity. Others are issues that will require both short-term strategies and longer-term recommendations.

Process for Analysis of Focus-Group Responses

After completion of the focus groups, the Best Practices Project's next challenge was to analyze the groups' responses. The commitment to an inclusive process required that the analysis capture examples of practice from the field in a manageable way while respecting the importance of the contribution of each focus group.

A subcommittee of the Best Practices Project Steering Committee, referred to as the Analysis Team (or A-Team), was formed to review some of the preliminary focus-group returns and direct the process. The project staff reviewed each response question by question to develop a comprehensive list of responses across focus groups. Responses were then reviewed program by program across all questions in order to obtain a holistic program perspective. Staff compared program responses from staff and family focus groups, looking for consistency in how staff and family participants viewed the program and its practice. Finally, a set of criteria was developed to select responses that represented examples of best practices. The majority of focus-group returns were reviewed and synthesized during March 1994. The work of "mining" the focus-group responses for examples of best practices continued as other sources of knowledge about practice were developed and examined. The commissioned papers, the literature review, and the ongoing consultation with practitioners, scholars, families, and advocates in family support added to the depth of knowledge about best practices in family support. The project continuously benefited from the wealth of experience and knowledge embodied in its steering committee. Other groups, such as the Coalition's African American and Latino caucuses and related projects of the Coalition, provided valuable and focused input into the effort to define best practices.

In March 1994, the Best Practices Project Steering Committee turned its attention to the task of revisiting the conceptual framework of the project. As important components of the Best Practices Project have become a reality, it has been and will continue to be important to further refine the interpretive framework for defining best practices in family support.

Next Steps in the Process of Defining Best Practices

At its March 1994 meeting, the Best Practices Project Steering Committee and project staff identified details of the next stages of the project. They recommended strategies for obtaining additional input on questions that were underrepresented in the focus-group process and which have not been thoroughly researched and documented in emerging literature. These strategies also served to secure additional participation and input from underrepresented groups. The strategies developed included:

1. Creating more opportunities for dialogue among representative groups of practitioners, families, and others around specific issues and within specific constituency groups (for example, maximizing opportunities for such dialogue to occur at the Coalition's 1994 national conference)

2. Targeting particular programs for telephone interviews and site visits

3. Developing short- and long-term strategies for continuous networking and relationship building with underrepresented groups

4. Developing recommendations for areas needing more

in-depth and, therefore, long-term inquiry and analysis

The A-Team met in June 1994 to review the information gathered from the wide spectrum of sources contributing to the process, and to begin work on the first draft of *Guidelines for Family Support Practice*.

The final stages of the Best Practices Project involved writing the manuscript. This was a collaborative effort in which co-authors Kathy Goetz Wolf and Judy Langford Carter relied on all of the materials that arose from previous stages of the process, convened groups of practitioners and others to flesh out difficult issues, and sought feedback on drafts from those in the field. Practice examples were gleaned from numerous telephone calls to programs and practitioners, thorough review of focus-group materials, and through other FRC documents, projects, and interviews. The final draft, following approval by the Best Practice Project Steering Committee, was reviewed and approved by the Coalition's Board of Directors.

The final stages of the project entail dissemination and consensus building. The objectives of consensus building are:

- To build a broad consensus on the content of *Guidelines for Family Support Practice*

- To help identify additional areas to explore in the form of addenda

- To encourage ownership of the outcome by diverse groups of program providers and other professionals

- To publicize the effort and its outcomes

The dissemination plan for the book includes continuing to expand networks and channels of communication by facilitating:

- Communication with the field through regular FRC channels [e.g., sending the book to FRC conference attendees who requested it; publicizing it in FRC newsletters; and using the framework and insights of the book in caucus communications, conference presentations, and technical assistance and consulting to local- and state-level programs and agencies]

- Communication with "network" organizations, i.e., the large number of national organizations with which

FRC collaborates on a regular basis

- Communication with policymakers and managers in schools and human service systems who are interested in the family support approach as a strategy for serving families

- Communication with the general public, including promotion of knowledge about quality programs in local communities and promotion of knowledge of systems change related to family support principles

The Coalition anticipates that the Best Practices Project will make an array of new resources and reference materials available for local family support programs to use in program development, including *Guidelines for Family Support Practice* and the commissioned papers. A self-assessment procedure for program development and enhancement may also be developed to build on the work of the Best Practices Project.

FRC will not consider the Best Practices Project complete until its outcomes are translated into useful action in the field. *Guidelines for Family Support Practice* will serve as a resource for professional education and pre-service training to prepare staff to work in family support programs. The Family Resource Coalition and others will build on *Guidelines* to establish high-quality family support staff development strategies. *Guidelines* also will have implications for larger systems incorporating family support into their work with families.

Adhering to a process that is guided by values of diverse participation and inclusiveness has proven at times to be a formidable challenge. The response from the field was more than four times what FRC anticipated. The process of synthesizing and analyzing the responses to the focus-group questionnaire has merited careful attention. The Coalition worked to balance the value of inclusiveness with the need to manage in a meaningful way the massive amount of documentation received.

The search for relevant knowledge challenged FRC to stretch the network of family support and find new ways of building relationships with others whose work may not be labeled "family support" or who are not yet a part of the family support "family."

Table 1
Numbers and Types of Focus-Group Sessions Conducted*

Type of Focus Group	Number of Programs Conducting	Total Number of Sessions
Family	1	1
Staff	19	19
Both staff focus groups and family focus groups	74	148**
Total	94	168

*Information in Table 1 pertains only to focus groups organized by single programs, which accounted for 168 of 210 focus-groups sessions. The remaining 42 were sponsored by programs in collaboration.
**Programs each sponsored one group of families and one of staff

Table 2
Region: Focus Group Sessions Per Geographic Region

Region	Sponsored by Single Program	Sponsored by Group of Programs
Northwest (MT, OR, WA)	7	4
Southwest (AZ, CO, OK, TX, UT)	6	0
Midwest (IL, IN, MI, MN, MO, NE, OH, WI)	34	11
Mid-Atlantic (MD, RI, VA)	6	1
Pacific (AK, CA, HI)	9	1
Northeast (CT, NH, NJ, NY, PA, VT)	21	2
Southeast (AL, FL, GA, KY, LA, MS, NC, SC, TN)	14	4
Canada	1	1
Not indicated	5	4

Table 3
Type of Community: Type of Area in which Families Represented in Program Live

Location	Number of Programs	Proportion of Programs
Mega-urban	14	15%
Urban	29	31%
Suburban	13	14%
Rural	18	19%
Mixed	18	19%
Not indicated	2	3%
Total	94	

THE BEST PRACTICES PROJECT

Table 4

Program Setting: Type of Service Delivery Site As Reported By Program

Setting*	Number of Programs
Community-based center	26
Social service agency	23
Homes of families	20
School	18
Day-care center	15
Church or synagogue	11
Hospital	10
Workplace	5
College or university	3
Mental health center	3
Library	1
Military	1
Museum	1
Prison	1
Not indicated	26

* Some single programs listed multiple settings.

Table 5

Economic Level of Families Represented in Program

Economic Level	Number of Programs	Proportion of Programs
Poverty	42	44%
Lower	9	9%
Middle	7	7%
High	0	0%
Multiple	28	29%
Not indicated	8	9%
Total	94	

GUIDELINES FOR FAMILY SUPPORT PRACTICE

Racial and Ethnic Breakdown: Programs in which a Racial/Ethnic Group Represents
More Than 50% of Population Served

Racial/Ethnic Group that Represents More than 50% of Population Served	Number of Programs	Proportion of Programs
Caucasian	54	56%
African American	13	14%
Latino	1	1%
Asian	2	2%
Native American	0	0%
None/not indicated	25	27%
Total	94	

Racial and Ethnic Breakdown: Programs in which a Racial/Ethnic Group Represents
More Than 25% of Population Served

Racial/Ethnic Group that Represents More than 25% of Population Served	Number of Programs	Proportion of Programs
Caucasian	62	65%
African American	22	23%
Latino	5	5%
Asian	3	3%
Native American	1	1%
None/not indicated	1	2%
Total	94	

Table 7

Issues Discussed by Staff Focus Groups

Number/Issue	Number of Single-Program Focus Groups	Proportion of Single-Program Focus Groups*
1. Building on family strengths/seeking support as a family strength	68	73%
2. Parents as program decision makers	28	30%
3. Confident and competent parenting	60	65%
4. Staff and parents as partners	64	69%
5. Families as resources	27	29%
6. Parents as advocates	19	20%
7. Services for all family members	58	62%
8. Parent education	48	52%
9. Cultural respect and diversity/program is community-based	30	32%
10. Program as bridge between families and other resources	49	53%
11. Voluntary participation in programs	25	27%
12. Staff development and training	26	28%
13. Program effectiveness and evaluation	17	18%

*Percentages are based on a total of 93 staff focus groups conducted by single programs.

Table 8

Issues Discussed by Family Focus Groups

Number/Issue	Number of Single-Program Focus Groups	Proportion of Single-Program Focus Groups*
1a. Building on family strengths	39	52%
1b. Seeking support as a family strength	51	68%
2. Parents as program decision makers	32	43%
3. Confident and competent parenting	57	76%
4. Staff and parents as partners	43	57%
5. Families as resources	31	41%
6. Parents as advocates	21	28%
7. Services for all family members	31	41%
8. Parent education	50	67%
9. Cultural respect and diversity/program is community-based	14	19%
10. Program as bridge between families and other resources	24	32%
11. Voluntary participation in programs	15	20%

*Percentages are based on a total of 75 family focus groups conducted by single programs.

GUIDELINES FOR FAMILY SUPPORT PRACTICE

The following pages contain copies of the principles and premises of family support that are suitable for reproduction. Family Resource Coalition both grants permission and encourages you to copy these pages and to share them with coworkers and other colleagues.

Premises of Family Support

1. Primary responsibility for the development and well-being of children lies within the family, and all segments of society must support families as they rear their children.

The systems and institutions upon which families rely must effectively respond to their needs if families are to establish and maintain environments that promote growth and development. Achieving this requires a society that is committed to making the well-being of children and families a priority and to supporting that commitment by allocating and providing necessary resources.

2. Assuring the well-being of all families is the cornerstone of a healthy society, and requires universal access to support programs and services.

A national commitment to promoting the healthy development of families acknowledges that every family, regardless of race, ethnic background, or economic status, needs and deserves a support system. Since no family can be self-sufficient, the concept of reaching families before problems arise is not realized unless all families are reached. To do so requires a public mandate to make family support accessible and available, on a voluntary basis, to all.

3. Children and families exist as part of an ecological system.

An ecological approach assumes that child and family development is embedded within broader aspects of the environment, including a community with cultural, ethnic, and socio-economic characteristics that are affected by the values and policies of the larger society. This perspective assumes that children and families are influenced by interactions with people, programs, and agencies as well as by values and policies that may help or hinder families' ability to promote their members' growth and development. The ecological context in which families operate is a critical consideration in programs' efforts to support families.

4. Child-rearing patterns are influenced by parents' understandings of child development and of their children's unique characteristics, personal sense of competence, and cultural and community traditions and mores.

There are multiple determinants of parents' child-rearing beliefs and practices, and each influence is connected to other influences. For example, a parent's view of her or his child's disposition is related to the parent's cultural background and knowledge of child development and to characteristics of the child. Since the early years set a foundation for the child's development, patterns of parent-child interaction are significant from the start. The unique history of the parent-child relationship is important to consider in programs' efforts.

5. Enabling families to build on their own strengths and capacities promotes the healthy development of children.

Family support programs promote the development of competencies and capacities that enable families and their members to have control over important aspects of their lives and to relate to their children more effectively. By building on strengths, rather than treating deficits, programs assist parents in dealing with difficult life circumstances as well as in achieving their goals, and in doing so, enhance parents' capacity to promote their children's healthy development.

6. The developmental processes that make up parenthood and family life create needs that are unique at each stage in the life span.

Parents grow and change in response to changing circumstances and to the challenges of nurturing a child's development. The tasks of parenthood and family life are ongoing and complex, requiring physical, emotional, and intellectual resources. Many tasks of parenting are unique to the needs of a child's developmental stage, others are unique to the parent's point in her or his life cycle. Parents have been influenced by their own childhood experiences and their own particular psychological characteristics, and are affected by their past and present family interactions.

7. Families are empowered when they have access to information and other resources and take action to improve the well-being of children, families, and communities.

Equitable access to resources in the community—including up-to-date information and high-quality services that address health, educational, and other basic needs—enables families to develop and foster optimal environments for all members. Meaningful experiences participating in programs and influencing policies strengthen existing capabilities and promote the development of new competencies in families, including the ability to advocate on their own behalf.

From: *Guidelines for Family Support Practice* (1996) (Chicago: Family Resource Coalition). **For more information or to obtain a copy of *Guidelines for Family Support Practice* contact the Family Resource Coalition, 200 S. Michigan Ave., 16th Floor, Chicago, IL 60604, phone: 312/341-0900, fax: 312/341-9361.**

Principles of Family Support Practice

1. Staff and families work together in relationships based on equality and respect.

2. Staff enhance families' capacity to support the growth and development of all family members—adults, youth, and children.

3. Families are resources to their own members, to other families, to programs, and to communities.

4. Programs affirm and strengthen families' cultural, racial, and linguistic identities and enhance their ability to function in a multicultural society.

5. Programs are embedded in their communities and contribute to the community-building process.

6. Programs advocate with families for services and systems that are fair, responsive, and accountable to the families served.

7. Practitioners work with families to mobilize formal and informal resources to support family development.

8. Programs are flexible and continually responsive to emerging family and community issues.

9. Principles of family support are modeled in all program activities, including planning, governance, and administration.

From: *Guidelines for Family Support Practice* (1996) (Chicago: Family Resource Coalition).

For more information or to obtain a copy of *Guidelines for Family Support Practice* contact the Family Resource Coalition, 200 S. Michigan Ave., 16th Floor, Chicago, IL 60604, phone: 312/341-0900, fax: 312/341-9361.

Notes

GUIDELINES FOR FAMILY SUPPORT PRACTICE

Spread the Word About This Book ...

If you are using *Guidelines for Family Support Practice* to:

- ◆ put family support principles into practice in your daily work,
- ◆ train others in working with families in the most empowering and supportive ways,
- ◆ plan and fund family support initiatives,
- ◆ set standards to strive for in delivering services to parents, or
- ◆ strengthen and support families in other ways,

then help introduce this important resource to others, so they can do the same!

and Get Another One Free.

Can you send the Family Resource Coalition a mailing list of people and agencies in your community or state that should have *Guidelines for Family Support Practice*? Would you like to sell the book through your catalog or at your site? Do you know of groups that want training in implementing family support?

There are many ways to help get this resource into the hands of family support practitioners, planners, funders, trainers, and researchers you know. When you do, FRC will send you a free copy of the *Companion Guide to Guidelines for Family Support Practice*, a ten-dollar value. It provides an executive summary of *Guidelines for Family Support Practice*, applies the guidelines to the work of various audiences who are concerned with the well-being of children and families, and recommends next steps for family-serving programs, policymakers, trainers, researchers, and evaluators.

Just fill out and return the form below! Or call FRC for more information at 312/341-0900.

Send Me My Free Companion Guide!

□ Enclosed is our mailing list.

□ We would like to sell *Guidelines for Family Support Practice*.

□ We would like training or know others who would.

Name (individual member or organization contact)   Title

Program/Organization   Phone

Organization Address (no P. O. boxes)   Fax

City/State/ZIP

Home Address

Home Phone

Send me more copies of *Guidelines for Family Support Practice*

Send ___ copies at $35 each,
$25 each for FRC members
Less 10% discount for five or more
Plus shipping and handling (see right)
TOTAL:

Card # _____

Exp. Date _____

Cardholder _____

Signature _____

Shipping and Handling

Book Total	UPS Shipping
$25 – 49.99	$5
$50 – 99.99	$7.50
$100 – 149.99	$10
$150 – 199.99	$15
$200 +	10% of total

Non–U.S. orders: Add 10% to above

Mail or fax to:
FAMILY RESOURCE COALITION   200 S. Michigan Avenue, 16th Floor   Chicago, IL 60604   312/341-9361 (fax)